I0004830

Simple Facebook Privacy

How to Reduce Your Risk Online

Russell Mickler

SIMPLE BOOKS

First Printing: September 2012. Version 1.3.

Written in the United States of America Between
October 2011 – September 2012

Prepared using Oracle OpenOffice ® 3.2 on Ubuntu 11.10
Times Font 10 pt

ISBN-13: 978-0-9835241-1-3
Amazon Print on Demand Version

Some of the material in this book, though revised and expanded,
originated on the author's blog.

Praise for *Simple Social Media*

"I needed a book that spoke to a social media challenged business owner. I found it. The book is very straight forward and talks a language that I can understand. I am using the principles presented in this book, and my Facebook page is growing and I actually know what I am doing."

— *Terry*, Amazon.com Review

"I liked Simple Social Media because it explained HOW I should be posting and/or blogging. It tells me when it is the most effective time to do it and on which days ... Russell Mickler uses a plain-English method of instruction that a business person can understand."

— *Isaac*, Amazon.com Review

"Russell has avoided the all too typical geek speak, and explains things in a clear and well researched book. He answers the questions we all have: "What's in it for me? Why should I use it? What is the return on my investment?" ... Simple Social Media is a must read if you want to understand what social media can do for you and how to get started properly."

— *Rusty*, Amazon.com Review

"If you're a web designer with your own business or work for a large company, this is a great book to read. It will help you fully understand social media and how to be successful at it. It will also help you come across more knowledgeable and should boost your confidence and increase your bottom line as a web entrepreneur."

— *Riley*, Amazon.com Review

"Mr. Russell Mickler is like the person in a corn maze that not only points the way, but escorts me personally through the maze. I am still in the very early stages; however I appreciate having this book as a guide."

- *Dr. Marc*, Amazon.com Review

DISCLAIMER

No patent liability is assumed with respect to the use of the information contained herein. Although every precaution has been taken in the preparation of this book, the publisher and author assume no responsibility for errors or omissions. Nor is any liability assumed for damages resulting from the use of information contained herein. Every effort has been made to make this book as complete and as accurate as possible, but no warranty or fitness is implied. The information is provided on an "as is" basis

.

PUBLISHER

SIMPLE BOOKS
13504 NE 84th Street, STE 103-150
Vancouver, Washington 98682
www.simple-books.net
Voice: 360.216.1784
Fax: 360.397.0468

ERRORS AND OMISSIONS

To report errors and omissions, please send a note to errata@simple-books.net.

COVER DESIGN

Chris Martin of Chris Martin Studios
www.chrismartinstudios.com

TRADEMARKS

All terms mentioned in this book that are known to be trademarks or service marks have been appropriately capitalized. Use of a term in this book should not be regarded as affecting the validity of any trademark or service mark.

BULK SALES

Simple Books offers discounts on this book when ordered in quantity for bulk purchases or special sales. For more information, please contact the publisher at booksales@simple-books.net.

MAILING LIST

Would you like to receive updates and information from Simple Books? Want to know when our special author events, signings, promotions, and seminars will be taking place? Then join our mailing list at http://www.simple-books.net/subscribe.

ABOUT THE AUTHOR

Russell Mickler, Principal Consultant of Mickler & Associates, Inc., has over 17 years of professional experience leading and managing IT organizations. As a technology consultant, Mickler assists small to mid-range businesses with crafting and executing technology strategy. In addition to earning his Master's Degree in technology from the University of Oregon, Mickler is a Computer Information Systems Security Professional (CISSP) and a Microsoft Certified Systems Engineer (MCSE). Mickler teaches graduate and undergraduate technology courses for many universities across the country. Mickler is the co-author of several books concerning Information Technology and Information Security. Mickler is also a public speaker on matters concerning social media and technology, and creates all types of media at micklerandassociates.com and his blog reinventwork.com. Russell Mickler and Mickler & Associates, Inc. can be found on Facebook, on Twitter at @micklerr, and emailed directly at russell@simple-books.net.

OTHER BOOKS AND PUBLICATIONS BY THE AUTHOR

Simple Social Media

READER FEEDBACK

It's my hope that you find this book useful and practical, and as my reader, you're the most important critic in the world. If you have comments or suggestions regarding this book, please feel free to send your ideas my way via email, Facebook, or online surveys. I'd love to receive your feedback.

READER SERVICES AND MATERIALS

Many materials, presentations, videos, and downloadable forms mentioned within this book can be found on the author's website, www.simple-books.net.

- To Regina, with whom all things are possible.

Contents

INTRODUCTION

Thanks again for picking up another Simple Book.

Regrettably, there are two problems I found in writing a book about Facebook Privacy.

First there's the nature of the subject matter. I mean, if you got a gaggle of nerds in a room and then opened the floor up for discussion, this issue could easily explode into a maelstrom of verbal geekery. Who'd want to read that?

Secondly, the speed of technical changes that can be adopted by Internet companies like Facebook is so rapid that keeping a writing schedule is a bit like chasing down moles in your backyard. You see evidence of the mole, you investigate, you document the mole's random path of destruction, and then to realize the mole's moved on to create a new hole and you must start all over. It's a global wack-a-mole moving at the speed of light.

Over the eight months I spent researching and writing this book, Facebook implemented Timelines and changed the way users interacted with their Profiles, forcing re-writes to numerous sections. Sprinkling a bit more salt into my wound was the twenty-year agreement Facebook reached with the FTC concerning privacy, and then, Zuckerberg had the audacity to take his company through an IPO and emerged as a publically-traded company.

Jesh, some people.

Like many things on the Internet, this issue is far from static, and it'll take years (potentially decades if we're to critically look at the FTC/Facebook timeline) to really nail down the issue. Facebook Privacy is inherently a complex and evolving issue and it was tough keeping pace with it. My challenge in writing this work was to make it approachable by anyone and relevant enough to be used as a field-guide for exploring big-picture security concepts, and, for modifying actual Facebook settings. I felt that the problem needed to first be defined on an abstract level and then followed-up with concrete safeguards. We needed to talk about big-picture ideas and still take specific forms of action. Therefore you'll find that the topics flow from really big, macro-sized concepts to small, micro-sized changes and settings you can implement today in Facebook.

I hope you find the book's structure and rather informal (often sarcastic and snarky) language approachable.

I wrote this book with you in mind - the enlightened consumer, the small business owner, the concerned parent, the inquisitive teenager, the critical grandparent – anyone who would like some ready-made tips for reducing their risks online using Facebook's service. Ultimately, the purpose of this work is to help you make better decisions that could prevent the compromise of Personal Private Information (PPI) that could be used as a means to conduct identity theft or fraud against you, your business, or your family. I believe anyone who is not technical can pick up this book, learn about the broad-stroke problems, and implement a tighter control in Facebook that makes their Facebook experience more secure tomorrow.

Risks concerning the privacy of social networks are a complicated issue that demands plain, clear speak in a language that everybody can understand. Just as Facebook is emerging from IPO and creating a virtual scrapbook for the entirety of our lives, I think now's a great time to have that conversation. This work encompasses many ideas from my thirteen years of teaching graduate and undergraduate technology curriculum, my eighteen years in the technology industry, and my professional licensing, certification, and training.

It's my contention that many of the problems facing privacy on Facebook has more to do with our own habits, behaviors, lack of understanding, and assumptions, and less than a failing of Facebook's software. No software is ever totally secure and Facebook will never realistically arrive at a point where they satisfy everyone with absolute confidence in their solution. Instead, what steps we take today to educate ourselves, change our habits, and how we go about implementing our own tighter controls is far more important than forcing Facebook to acknowledge its platform and policy weaknesses. What's important now is assuming personal responsibility and enacting a reasonable set of responses. And that's what I hope to show you in the book.

Thanks for reading.
R

The Business of Social Networks

What You Will Learn

- What are social networks?
- What do the terms *security* and *privacy* mean?
- You and your personal private information (PPI) are a product
- Facebook's track-record in preserving your PPI
- Why Facebook isn't the enemy

What are Social Networks?

Social networks are a destination on the Internet. They're places where people hang out online. They can create user accounts and login to chat, play games, upload content like pictures and status updates, share social media, and interact with their friends. They're a huge time-suck. Between their computers and mobile devices, Americans spend more than 22-percent of their online time on social networks.[1]

Facebook is just such a social network and undoubtedly you've heard of it before. You're likely already a member, at least, that's what I'm assuming. There are many social networks spread all around the world but Facebook is the Big Kahuna of them all. Facebook has over 900 million active users and more than fifty percent of its user community will login to Facebook on any given day.[2]

When examining user adoption and the number of registered users, Facebook is twice as large as Qzone, China's social network; six times bigger than Twitter; seven-times bigger than Linked-In; and more than twenty-times larger than Google+.[3] Facebook is *the name* in social networks. They even made a movie about it. Wow.

While logged-in to social networks, users are encouraged to share a lot of information about themselves. They're invited to share because that's what being *social* is all about. Facebook encourages its users to share their backgrounds, education, and work history; share their preferences for music, art, entertainment, and politics; share their opinions on brands, products, and services; share their media like pictures, audio-clips, and blog posts; they play games, answer surveys, and engage in discussions, all-the-while indirectly sharing information about them. Share, share, and share some more. Social networks are designed to help users effortlessly share their everyday experiences while interacting with their online friends. Social networks are all about *sharing*.

On Facebook, users share content with their friends and, as you know, a *friend* on Facebook is somewhat of a euphemism. A Facebook friend is an association made to another registered Facebook user that says: "I *trust* this person enough to *share* my ideas, content, and preferences with them." One person might have ten, twenty, eighty, or even hundreds of friends, most of which they wouldn't know from Adam if they were to meet in real-life; if you were curious, the average Facebook user has 130 friends.[4] Still, a vast majority of Facebook friends aren't really "friends" at all but are probably people you didn't want to offend by not *friending* them in the first place – perhaps a rather dubious distinction for considering them worthy for *sharing* and *trust*.

Yet consumers are not alone on the Facebook landscape. Businesses and brands also camp-out on social networks to better engage with their customers. Businesses also want to *share* and they also want to be *trusted* by the consumer. If they can become a trusted participant in the conversation then consumers are more likely to buy from them, recommend them, or promote them online, so there's also a commercial aspect to being a friend.

On Facebook, people are *friends*; businesses are *friends*; producers and consumers are *friends*; celebrities and politicians are *friends*; all manner of objects, places, and things are *friends*. All of these associations create links between people, brands, companies, preferences, and tastes that take up *petabytes* of data storage – just mounds and mounds of data. As my hero Jack Nicholson might say, "It's all just so freekin' friendly."

And best of all, Facebook is free. Free for everyone to use anywhere. But how can that be? I mean, critically: how can a commercial enterprise as complex as Facebook, beholden to public shareholders and private investors, give away software and services for free? How can Facebook allow politicians, celebrities, and businesses nearly constant and direct access to constituents, fans, and consumers without some form of compensation?

- Does the personal fortune of Facebook's CEO and creator Mark Zuckerberg somehow provide for an ambitious, altruistic new model of Capitalism that doesn't expect any conventional return on investment?

- Does Facebook operate at zero-expenses?

- Are Facebook budgets filled with public tax-dollars?

- Do the employees of Facebook donate their time as volunteers?

No. No, no, and no.

Social networks exist to collect information about consumers and companies like Facebook make money from reselling that information as a product, or, as a means to direct targeted forms of advertising.

You see, social networks are an amazingly-rich data mine. Hugely rich. Data collected by Facebook are some of the most comprehensive compilations of consumer facts, tastes, behaviors, buying decisions, and opinions found anywhere on the planet. This data can collectively be seen as the Personal Private Information (PPI) of consumers that is handed over voluntarily in the course of interacting with their friends on Facebook.

So Facebook is in the friendly game of *sharing*, too. Facebook just doesn't store the PPI of consumers. Facebook *shares* the PPI of consumers. On Facebook, private owner-operators of private websites register to be authorized third-parties to Facebook, and registered third-parties can get access to Facebook's data repository. Software frameworks like Facebook's Open Graph allow third parties to create a more "personalized" experience of their own website borrowing from PPI stored by Facebook.[5]

Using Open Graph, third-parties can ask Facebook about you, write applications that impersonate you, extract data about you, and learn more about your preferences and behaviors. When users play games like Farmville, or take quizzes, listen to music, share a picture, chat, or generate a cute graphic representing their top-ten friends, read a book, or watch a movie, they're authorizing an application written by third-parties access to their Facebook Profile: the central place where users keep their PPI.

What Happens to My PPI on Facebook?

Facebook manages the data they collect in massive computer facilities around the world called data centers. These are highly-complex spaces of computer systems and digital storage equipment that requires professional management around-the-clock. Abstractly, companies like Facebook would refer to this architecture as their *cloud* – a notion of interconnected software and computing devices that run the Facebook software on computers, cell phones, tablet computers, everywhere around the globe - managed by trained professionals who're hired or contracted by Facebook. And Facebook spends an extraordinary amount of time, man-hours, and resources in their cloud to protect it – making the data redundant, secure, and accurate. After all, all of that cool data is an asset to them. It's what makes Facebook money.

You Are the Product

Now maybe you've heard of the old adage, "If something is free then you are the product"? Yup. On Facebook, you are the product. Its services are free and that's important: membership fees would create barriers to adoption. Social networks are engineered to capture data about consumers so it's easier to market to them. Little pieces of you, captured over time, are – in effect – the asset of social network companies, and through signing-up and using the service for free you've voluntarily agreed to surrender your PPI into their custody.

Custody is a key word here. Facebook would probably like to refer to itself as a humble *custodian* of your PPI. A professional, benevolent actor whose diligence, expertise, and technology foresight protects your PPI from being lost, stolen, hacked, or abused by them or by the third-parties they share your PPI with.

The word *custodian*, however, implies a *caretaker* role where this function is provided devoid of agenda and personal gain, yet that isn't really what's happening. Facebook is more like a *curator*, a collector, who then resells what they've accumulated to others for profit. Facebook's cloud can track activities on the Internet outside of Facebook itself, and relate those activities back to their users: what they saw, what they watched, what they liked or disliked, what they felt, where they were … exponentially extending the value of their asset with each and every passing day. Facebook is a curator of a very rich collection of consumer preferences, preoccupations, and proclivities to such an extent that would otherwise seem rather Orwellian if it were in the hands of a government.

There Ought to be a Law

But Facebook is not the government. It's a public company and contrary to what you might initially believe what Facebook does is not illegal. When you sign-up for a Facebook account, you give implicit permission to Facebook to capture your information, store it, and share it with third-parties via its End User License Agreement (EULA). Perhaps you weren't aware of Facebook's Privacy Policies and other conditions that you agreed to when signing-up? Facebook assumes that every user has read them. Surely you've read them. Well, haven't you? Oh, if you haven't, I'd highly encourage that you do:

https://www.facebook.com/about/privacy/your-info#howweuse.

Understandably, like most end-users of digital services on the Internet, you've not made it a common practice to read every EULA and privacy policy you're presented with but more to the point: there's no law in the United States that mandates protection over the kind of information collected by Facebook. There is one exception in the case of children under the age of fourteen which is, by the way, the reason why Facebook doesn't allow anyone younger than fourteen to sign-up for Facebook; doing so would require Facebook to tighten its PPI controls concerning children.[6]

Facebook and Third Parties

In their privacy policy, Facebook says that it will share your PPI with third parties and other companies by which they've a business relationship. Examples:

- Facebook may provide information to service providers to help bring you Facebook services at their websites. Stuff like your picture, comments, information from Facebook can be pulled from Facebook by third parties.

- Third parties to Facebook may read your profile contents to target specific forms of advertising to you while you're using Facebook.

- Facebook may be required to disclose some information due to lawful requests such as subpoenas and court orders without notice. They may also share your PPI with law enforcement, lawyers, companies, or agents when Facebook feels it's necessary or important to protect their interests or property.

- Ownership of your PPI would transfer to a new owner should Facebook fail.

- Facebook may change, alter, or destroy your PPI without notice at any time but they do honor Title 17 (Copyright) restrictions and have a grievance procedure.

Within their guidelines, Facebook indemnifies itself from:

- The security and privacy practices of the third parties they associate with; they clearly state they aren't responsible for the privacy policies or the way their partners interact with you while you're online;

- Facebook isn't responsible for incorrect or inaccurate information posted as user content;

- They're not responsible for the conduct of any user while using their service;

- Facebook assumes no responsibility for errors, omissions, interruptions, deletions, defects, or delays in transmission of user content or communications;

- Facebook isn't responsible for your computer, its hardware or software, or the telecommunications you employ;

- Facebook isn't responsible for losses, damages, personal injury, or death, in any way related to the use of their service – it's provided "as-is" – and Facebook isn't financially responsible to anyone.

Again, it's important to understand that Facebook indemnifies itself from liability should your information be inappropriately used or collected; it can share anything about you at any time with anyone.

Is Facebook the Enemy?

Well, in a word, no.

Facebook isn't a bad company by any means, nor a morally or ethically corrupt organization. Facebook isn't the enemy. Facebook provides a service desired by their users. Facebook provides the kind of customization and personalization across the Internet desired by their users. Facebook offers support and responds to complaints from its users. Facebook is a legitimate enterprise that is reasonably transparent, takes reasonable precautions to protect its data centers, and reasonably manages the data entrusted in their care. As compared to similar companies who conduct similar practices, their procedures are verifiably equal and perhaps exceedingly transparent given their relative stature as the biggest social network. They are the constant target of scrutiny and investigation by the computer industry. Facebook is managed like any other corporation and must follow Federal and state laws concerning the management of their company, pay taxes, report earnings and expenses to the SEC, and remain accountable to a wide array of communications authorities.

All things considered, I'd try to convince you that Facebook shouldn't be demonized. Facebook isn't nefarious and evil. Facebook isn't busily using the PPI of its users to forge checks, launder money, or hock consumer phone numbers and addresses wholesale. Facebook is simply a clever company that has capitalized off the merger of computers, telephony, and the Internet. Facebook does a good job providing what their customers want - bearing in mind that you and I aren't necessarily a *customer* to Facebook - and they take reasonable efforts to safeguard the PPI they collect. Facebook, you see, isn't necessarily the problem.

Unfortunately, our adversaries are a little less obvious.

Our problem is the over-aggressive marketer, programmer, hacker, phreaker, phisher, malware, smisher, scam artist, fraudster, and other sorts of unscrupulous oddfellows who'd use Facebook compromise our user accounts. We've got a third-party problem. Once consumer PPI has been extracted from Facebook, these parties may proceed to use such data outside of Facebook's terms and conditions, and may attempt to direct contact you, spam you, conduct identity theft, commit fraud, stalk you, commit a crime, or carry out malicious activity against your computer.

Facebook is like the ring-master of a circus standing on an elevated podium to address an amassing crowd, "*Come one, come all, to the greatest show on Earth!*" All are drawn to the spectacle. We enter the tent and find it fun and intriguing, and will even make Facebook a frequent activity in our day. Yet among the crowd of spectators are thieves, pick-pockets, and snake-oil salesmen who'd use Facebook and the mass of people it's gathered as an opportunity to trick honest patrons unaware. And such is the security challenge for Facebook. Facebook has to convince users their software is safe and inspire confidence to keep them socializing online.

What is Security?

By this time, you've hopefully accepted that social networks are a means of collecting consumer PPI for advertisers as a form of entertainment, and hopefully I've convinced you that social networks of all stripes – not just Facebook – pose a significant risk to your personal privacy, and hopefully you're interested in learning more about how you can ratchet-up your security settings on Facebook to strengthen your privacy.

Well, I should hope so. That's what this book is about. Security, though, is a funny term with many definitions to different people and it deserves a conversation.

Security is more a subjective measure than an objective measure. What I mean is that security is just a *feeling*. It's a *feeling* you and I have in the confidence we've placed in our safeguards – the steps we've taken to protect ourselves.

Let's take your home as an example. Some might feel perfectly secure in a house with a locked front door secured only by a deadbolt. You might even think that's reasonable yourself and that you'd feel relatively secure. Still, others might look at that as an entirely insufficient precaution. They'd require an alarm, bars across the windows, motion detection, flood lights, a fence, and two Doberman Pinschers poised on the front lawn.

So which one is more secure? Is it the one who spent the most money? Would adding a camera system, a moat, and some alligators make it more secure? How do you know? What's threatening them? Are dogs really relevant if the owner has more to fear from a tornado or a flood?

And this is why the term *security* is so elusive. Security isn't a black and white concept. It represents a feeling based on the steps we've taken to protect ourselves. Fact: two rational people could look at the threats that confront them and conclude separate courses of action whereas both are equally legitimate and both parties feel secure in their choices. Thus Facebook thinks you're secure. It's taken reasonable precautions. It's locked the dead-bolt.

Your aunt feels secure on Facebook.

Your buddies on Facebook think they're secure.

And you might feel otherwise.

Feelings are not static, perfect, or absolute. Threats change over time so our safeguards have to be routinely assessed for suitability. There's no perfect defense against an evolving, ever-changing threat from unscrupulous partners to Facebook who desire access to our PPI. So, if security is simply a feeling, you might ask yourself, "How am I feeling today? What have I done to ensure the privacy of my own PPI? What have I done to limit my exposure? How am I managing the risks I'm facing online?"

If you're unsure and really can't answer those questions, if you feel somewhat of a pit in your stomach about now, then you're in a state of *insecurity*. You don't know. You really can't know. You don't have confidence in your safeguards because you've done nothing deliberate to manage your risk. At best, this emotional state could make you anxious and fearful, and perhaps determined to do something about it – hey, thanks for reading! Worse, it might make you ignorant, naïve, and apathetic. Meh, nothing will happen to you, right? You're nigh-invulnerable.

Regrettably, you're not. Your security is directly proportionate to the steps you've taken to protect your online privacy and is indirectly related to the software safeguards introduced by Facebook. To feel more secure, you're going to have to take additional action; you're going to have to assume personal responsibility for understanding the risks and for implementing safeguards.

What is Privacy?

Now, in the context of social networking, privacy is the idea that we should be free from observation or disruption from others. It also eludes that we should be able to conceal confidential information about ourselves. Facebook prescribes to a "default-opt-in" privacy policy. When you join Facebook or should Facebook add new features, it's assumed by Facebook that you'd like to take advantage of it. Facebook makes an assumption. The assumption is that you wish to share your content to the public and make it available to everybody. Should you disagree with the social network's assumption then you must deliberately "opt-out" by locating a specific software setting to change it. Facebook has been highly criticized for its "default-opt-in" policies.

At Facebook's defense, this isn't necessarily malicious behavior, either. The owner-operator of a social network doesn't necessarily conceal the *defacto* opt-in yet doesn't go out of its way to refer users to specific places to turn these settings off; let's remember that public participation and new content rewards them. That's what the network exists for: to be *social*, to *share*. The default opt-in presumption serves Facebook well. If everyone went about changing their settings, Facebook wouldn't have a product to sell, and that runs contrary to Facebook's function. Still, Facebook must respond to our *feelings* of insecurity and provide us with some control over its software to limit exposure. Certainly you can see the conflict of interest. What a catch-22!

A Right to Privacy

Often I've heard privacy advocates talk about certain "rights" on social networks and I believe they operate from a total misunderstanding of the law. There is no right to privacy in the United States – in fact, it's quite opposite: the First Amendment to the US Constitution grants the freedom for anybody to say whatever they please about somebody else. The only

Constitutional provision for confidentiality comes from the Fourth Amendment and its intention is to exclude illegally-seized evidence from being admitted in court. It has nothing to do with our commercial dealings as producers and consumers.

Turning then towards the Legislative Branch of our government, federally, laws have been introduced that protects certain classifications of consumer information and deems them as being *private* – most notably the educational transcripts of students (FERPA), the PPI of under-aged minors (COPPA), confidential financial information (Gramms-Leach-Bliley), and the insurance and private health information of consumers (HIPAA)[7]; whereas state privacy laws generally address video and wiretapping, computer crime, credit reporting, employee and insurance records, genetic information, and telemarketing solicitation.[8]

Still, none of these have anything to do with what you might tell someone in a public square, or, share with someone on a survey you voluntarily submitted to, or a game we signed up to play, or a message we shouted over a bullhorn. Whether or not you're in a physical public square or an electronic one like Facebook, what is voluntarily said in a public space is presumed to have no expectation of privacy whatsoever. Such content is by definition *public*. There's no such thing as a *right* to Privacy in this country let alone on Facebook, and aside from assuming the risk of slander, libel, or nuisance, anybody has almost absolute freedom to collect information about anybody else and do whatever they want with it.

In 1998, the Federal Trade Commission published a report to Congress entitled Privacy Online, identifying the five "widely adopted fair principles of online privacy: Notice, Choice, Access, Security, and Redress."[9] Facebook implements fair principles through:

Notice. Facebook notifies a user about its practices through its Privacy Policy. Many Facebook users may not read them but they're there.

Choice. Facebook offers its users Account Settings and Privacy Settings that allow the user to decide what PPI to share and with whom. Many Facebook users may not be aware of those choices and they're set to the most public access possible by default, but they are available.

Access. Facebook allows users to access information about themselves and change that information at will. Many Facebook users want to easily share PPI with friends and are unclear how much PPI is shared with others.

Security. Facebook is very vague about its security precautions it is presumed that Facebook takes reasonable precautions in securing the data it collects about consumers. Facebook offers its users one factor of identification (a username and password) to secure their PPI, and through its Privacy Settings users can restrict what content can be uploaded and tagged in their name by other users. Again, most users are unaware of these options or the risks they face by being a user.

Redress. Facebook must employ means to catch violations to its Privacy Policy and provide for appropriate means of recourse by injured parties. Facebook offers a section in their Help to Report Abuse or Policy Violations. Sadly, it'd be my presumption that Facebook users barely know this page exists or when to use it.

So Should We Presume Social Networks to be Private?

Inherently, social networks are *social*.

For me, advocating privacy on Facebook an incoherent argument. It's kind of like an introverted person who sincerely desired to be a recluse consciously chose to drive to a crowded town square so they can hang-out, talk to people, share intimate details about their lives, and play games with others, then they get mad because they're being pestered, annoyed, shocked, or concerned that people are sharing too much.

Seriously: why are they there in the first place? It's a *social* network. In my opinion, there's no inherent expectation of privacy in a social network. They are what they are. They're designed to effortlessly capture consumer information and make it available to others and it's paid for through the voluntarily surrender of PPI. That's how it works.

When privacy advocates cry foul whenever Facebook provides a new feature or enhancement *to do what it's designed to do*, I think one should look at their objections with a bit of rational skepticism. Facebook isn't designed to be private. It's designed to *share*! With every new release or feature, Facebook provides value to a user community who expects their tool to consume ideas, pictures, videos, thoughts, to share and to entertain. If privacy advocates were even vaguely sincere they'd simply cancel their account immediately. Obviously, they should join a *private* network; *social* networks just aren't for them.

Inasmuch, this would be a good first question to ask yourself. Knowing what you know about Facebook and their business model, is being on Facebook right for you? If the perceived risks outweigh the perceived benefits, perhaps not; you may be convinced to close your account right away. There's no shame in that. Put down the book and go get that done. Otherwise, if you find value in the service, you may be interested in how to limit your exposure and control your Personal Private Information to the greatest extent offered by their software. That's what the rest of our discussion will involve.

Why Should You Take Action

What You Will Learn

- Some of the more public problems Facebook has had in securing PPI on their website
- The problem of identity theft in America and how it relates to social networks and data breaches
- Who's to blame?
- The twelve most important pieces of PPI you own
- Why there'll never be a magic pill that solves all of our privacy and security problems online

Facebook's Privacy Blunders

If I were to be asked if reasonable precautions could be taken to safeguard privacy and increase Facebook security, sure, I think the answer is yes, although recent figures released from Facebook don't necessarily inspire confidence.

Facebook estimated in October 2011 that over 600,000 Facebook accounts are compromised every single day[10] and over five million accounts experience excessive spamming.[11]

In June 2010, quite embarrassingly, Facebook employees were able to deliberately compromise their security model in a public test of impenetrability.[12] Woops.

But wait! That's not all.

I don't think it's unreasonable to take an honest look at publicized problems with Facebook's security and privacy in recent years:

- Facebook had security holes that made it possible for users to read their friends private chats[13]

- In May 2011, it was reported that the PPI of all of Facebook's 500 million users had been leaked to third-party companies[14]

- In February 2011, Facebook implemented a facial recognition feature that tags user profiles in uploaded photos[15]

- A hacker was found selling compromised Facebook usernames and passwords for $25 and $45 apiece[16]

- Facebook created and deployed an advertising platform called Beacon which automatically updated user profiles with their purchases and provided advertiser information – Beacon is now turned off[17]

- Facebook's terms and conditions were changed to afford Facebook exclusive ownership of user content[18]

- The implementation of Facebook Places allows for geolocation data to be tied back to individuals through their user profile[19]

- Facebook has a common practice of making privacy the exception rather than the default[20]

- Facebook announced in 2011 to create an entire timeline of its users lives available to all[21]

Well, okay, the stats aren't tremendously inspiring but as Forest Gump would say, "Facebook is as Facebook does." I believe we can look at most of these circumstances as a natural outcome of what Facebook is.

- Facebook is a *social* network. There should be no presumption of privacy.

- Facebook is one of the most important destinations on the Internet. Thus, consumers spend a lot of time there. That's very attractive to aggressors.

- Facebook's default security setting will always be *opt-in*.

- Privacy on Facebook grains against their purpose and their revenue model.

- More exposed PPI raises the opportunity for more identity theft and fraud.

So can Facebook do better? Absolutely. I'd even suggest the attention they've received over their public blunders has afforded Facebook an opportunity to examine its culture, adjust its policies, and make stronger programmatic changes. Nothing inspires corporations quite like media and regulatory scrutiny.

Still, I think it'd be a real mistake to consider Facebook a 100-percent secure and responsible custodian of consumer PPI. Facebook isn't perfect. Facebook makes mistakes. Facebook inadvertently permits third-parties access to stuff they shouldn't have access to. So short of my earlier recommendation of cancelling your Facebook account, I feel you should take reasonable precautions to protect your privacy.

Identity Theft in America

Now let's consider *why* you should do something about protecting your PPI; let's explore *why* you should aggressively seek to protect your privacy online. Indeed, why should you take some of the safeguards identified in this book? Why should you take the risks seriously?

Identity theft involves crime where PPI was used to compromise the financial and social reputation of others. Obviously we can't have a rational discussion about social networks without also considering some of the ramifications of identity theft in America. In 2010:

- 8.1 million Americans were victimized by Identity Theft amounting in $37 billion total losses

- 71% of fraud happens within a week of stealing a victim's personal data[22]

- There were 407 reported incidents of data breach resulting in 26 million exposed records[23]

- The average out-of-pocket expense for identity theft victims was $631[24]

- Consumers are 8-times more likely to be a victim of identity theft if they're part of a data breach[25]

- We can expect more in 2011 because of a dramatic increase in data breaches in the first quarter
- Friendly Fraud – where crimes are committed by friends are loved ones - increased by 7% in 2010 and represents 14-percent of all fraud[26]

- The FTC announced that identity theft ranked number one for the eleventh consecutive year on their list of top consumer complaints – of 1,339,265 complains in 2010, 19-percent were about identity theft[27]

Data breaches are incidents where PPI is acquired through hacking and system compromise, accidental loss of confidentiality, or negligence. Small companies, big companies, medium-sized companies, micro-businesses, mega-corporations, and even huge social networking companies like Facebook will lose control of consumer PPI. It happens. Often, they might witness a suspicious circumstance in their systems yet be incapable of accounting for questionable behavior. Computers are like that. And the statistics here imply that consumers are eight-times more likely to be a victim of identity theft if their PPI was involved in a data breach.

Astutely, you might see the direct correlation between data breaches and identity theft. Pay attention to that *eight-times* number. That's a big factor. A single incident relates to an eight-fold increase in risk.

Then consider that it is Facebook's purpose to collect and share information about you with small companies, big companies, medium-sized companies, micro-businesses, mega-corporations … it's their *business*

- Facebook doesn't necessarily have a stellar performance record in this area;

- As Facebook grows, it will obtain more capital to purchase software and equipment to collect, report, and offer more data on its core product (you);

- As Facebook grows, it becomes a principle repository for consumer PPI on the web, shaping consumer preferences and offering stronger integration from third-party websites;

- Third parties will use Facebook's integration to obtain more data about you;

- As your social network grows and you tack-on more friends, the more information they're likely to inadvertently collect and share about you with those third-parties;

- All the while, substantially increasing the risk of data breach from Facebook or any of its third-party partners;

- Whereas even one incident of breach exposes you eight-times over to identity theft.

Yikes!

Okay, So How Does Data Breach Happen?

A data breach is a technical phenomenon signaling the loss of control over an information system. That loss of control potentially exposes consumer PPI to an unauthorized aggressor who could potentially use the information to commit identity theft.

What's most concerning is the rapidity by which the aggressor can compromise the digital accounts owned by the victim. For instance, if a hacker is to obtain your Social Security Number, mailing address, phone number, and your birth date, they could use this information to potentially compromise your social network, your banking system, apply for credit, or impersonate you within just a few hours. All of the hacker's tools are online. They may even be accessed on a mobile device. In effect, a single data breach begets the risk of exponentially more instances of data breach, exposing the victim to an increasing level of vulnerability in such short timeframes that they're incapable of preventing it.

Making matters worse, many data breaches go unreported because consumers may not recognize them and small businesses do not know if their computer systems are secure. Neither have the investigatory or technical knowledge to ascertain if PPI has been compromised, and even if they did, most small businesses are unaware of the 31 separate state laws in the United States governing consumer notification. Aside from the career-ending embarrassment, they wouldn't know how to go about notifying consumers of a breach anyway. They're unaware of the law. They're unaware of their circumstances and vulnerability. It's a vicious, unregulated cycle.

Who Can Hurt Us?

You've probably heard of computer programs like viruses and malware that are deliberately written to exploit our personal private information. You've also been exposed to scary-sounding types of fraudsters who're Hell-bent on compromising our personal computer systems: hackers, phreakers, smishers, phishers, pharmers, botherders … they exist in our imagination like modern-day ogres, trolls, and hobgoblins, lurking somewhere in the dark digital forest.

These are the things that go bump in the night and culturally we've become so fixated on the problems of viruses, malware, and hackers that we've lost sight of the most dangerous threats involving the people we trust. People. People who know us, who understand us, who understand our vulnerabilities, expectations, and motivations; people like our employees; like our employers; like our vendors and contractors; like our partners, wives, husbands, and extended family. By far, people who we know and trust are more of a risk to us than any of these automatons and fanciful creatures that exist somewhere, out there.

And on Facebook, we're surrounded by *people*. People we theoretically trust. Oh, woops, wait a minute: people we trust only because we didn't want to offend them by not *friending* them. Okay, that could be a problem. Friendly fraud is a classification of identity theft where somebody we know exploited our PPI to their advantage. According to a 2004 report prepared by the Congressional Committee on Ways and Means, 50-percent of identity theft and fraud is committed by someone the victim knows.[28] and now you should consider how many people you've *friended* on Facebook. You can look at an increased number of "friends" being equivalent to an increased risk of exposure to identity theft.

Social Networking and Identity Theft

That said, using social media and social networks doesn't automatically increase instances of identity theft. It's not a fact that more friends on Facebook equals greater a propensity for crime. Instead, the numbers increase vulnerability. It simply makes the practice of identity theft easier and faster.

Low-tech methods for stealing PPI are still the most popular but this is an evolving problem. In 2009, stolen wallets and physical documents accounted for 43-percent of all reported incidents of identity theft while online methods accounted for only 11-percent. Still, it is becoming increasingly easier for a would-be party who wishes to aggressively use social networks as a means to compromise our PPI. Participation in social networks increase the potential for crimes of opportunity.

The facts are startling.

- PC World reported that a third of social network users have at least three pieces of PPI posted to their profiles that could lead to identity theft[29]

- Eighty-percent of those polled were concerned about privacy, yet almost sixty-percent were unaware of their privacy settings[30]

- Over a third of social networks admitted that they use the same password for all social networking accounts.[31]

- People who have used social media for over five years or more are two times as likely to become victims of identity theft[32]

- A Javelin Strategy and Research study learned that 36-percent of people over the age of 65 do not use privacy settings on social networks, yet they are the highest age-group for fraud[33]

Who Is To Blame?

Okay, so again, who is to blame? Who should be held accountable for under-reporting data breaches and for not taking corrective action to safeguard consumer PPI? It turns out that there's a lot of blame to spread around. The reality is that consumers, government, and businesses are all the blame because somebody has to make inconvenient choices to affect real change.

Government

- To date, the federal government has failed to create a universal data breach notification law that would compel businesses of all sizes to report these incidents.

- The federal government has also failed to implement a universal data management requirement for consumer PPI.

- Instead, there are a patch-work of inconsistent laws and practices spread across 31 states that make it very difficult to regulate and for businesses to understand their compliance obligation.

Consumers

- Generally speaking, consumers are apathetic, ignorant, lazy, and convenience-minded towards securing their PPI.

- Generally speaking, consumers demonstrate foolish behaviors and are slow to adopt preventative measures to safeguard themselves from identity theft.

- Generally speaking, consumers are hesitant to report crimes involving family and people they know.

Businesses

- 80-percent of businesses in the United States are small businesses.

- Most small businesses aren't aware of their compliance status or requirements because they don't have the technical talent, knowledge, or expertise.

- Very few audit their technology processes for vulnerability and implement corrective actions.

As you can see, there's not a single party that could be held responsible for the problems associated with data breach and companies like Facebook shouldn't be exclusively targeted as digital pariah. It's not Facebook's fault alone. All of these parties are accountable to some degree but ultimately there is only one person that is going to take the necessary corrective action to limit your vulnerability online, and that's you.

You.

So let's stop the blame-game. Let's take off the rose-colored glasses. Let's look at what's real. It's your responsibility to take reasonable precautions to protect your PPI or even opt-out of social networking all-together if you're intolerant of risk. You have to take responsibility by assessing your own vulnerability, by cataloging what you're exposed to, and you can start by understanding what a potential aggressor wants from you.

The 12 Most Important Things About You

When it comes to Facebook, I like to have conversations with students that describe what fraudsters and hackers wish to find. They can use automation and tools to breach Facebook security, gather specific pieces of PPI that would allow them to commit identity theft, and infiltrate your other online accounts. Here are the12 most valuable things about you fraudsters will look for on Facebook.

Your Full Name

A full name is useful in forging contracts and birth certificates. Avoid revealing your middle name on Facebook or other social networking sites.

Your Social Security Number

A Social Security Number (SSN) is the gateway to a thousand possibilities for a hacker. It's the proverbial golden ticket. A SSN will open employment records, tax records, education transcripts, credit reports, applications for bank accounts and financial securities, and so on. SSN's are not asked for on Facebook except in circumstances where Facebook is extending credit or making payments.

Your State Driver's License

The driver's license is the gold-standard for being able to vouch for your identity. It doesn't matter which state the license originates from. It's a coveted artifact attesting to who you are, and the worst thing about it is that it never changes. A driver's license number often remains the same forever making it extremely easy to extort and replicate. Facebook doesn't directly ask for your driver's license and you should be hesitant to provide it if you were ever asked for it.

Your Date of Birth

Your birthday is another great piece of information that's consistent across multiple computer systems and it's really easy to get on Facebook. Many social networks present the date of birth (DOB) conveniently within a user's profile. DOB's are often used in challenge questions to verify identities and rotate passwords.

Your Mother's Maiden Name

Another easily-obtained piece of information from Facebook is the maiden name of your mother. It's easy because Facebook conveniently draws a relationship between you, your mother, and her family, and it doesn't take a computer scientist to figure out the rest. Your mother's maiden name is used as a means of challenging the ownership of accounts and to rotate passwords.

A Password

Humans are generally lazy creatures of convenience and predictability. Once a hacker figures out just one password, statistics suggest that same password will be used across multiple websites. Maybe they're vary slightly – password1, password2, password3 – or they'll be the names of pets, children, hobbies, or interests. If the hacker can figure out just one password, they've got a 90-percent chance that the rest of passwords used by the user will be something just like it.

The Names of Children

And here again, Facebook makes this information extraordinarily easy to find. The names of our children and their DOB's is extraordinarily useful. Does it suggest that people on Facebook have nefarious intentions to, say, kidnap or exploit children? Unlikely. But the names and DOB's of children make exceptionally easy passwords for people to remember, and the hacker knows that Facebook can be a source of this information.

Utility Bills and Statements

Combined with a driver's license or SSN, a utility bill can allow a potential fraudster to appear as whomever they please. If you're desiring to reinvent yourself or impersonate others, all you need is a legitimate utility bill that supposedly proves where you live; another great reason to own a paper shredder. Listen, in the shady world of poverty, desperation, a scarcity, things like Utility Bills are used as a mechanism of last resort to verify residency because it's the only tangible form of confirmation that somebody might be able to muster, and it could be as easy as "dumpster-diving" your trash can to assume your identity. And, oh yes, your address is on Facebook.

A Previous Address

When attempting to conduct some manner of business over the telephone, often a confirming party will look to verify your identity using a previous address. They can do this because old addresses will appear on a credit report. If a hacker is able to get just one of these, perhaps two, then that may be enough to convince the confirming party that they are who they claim to be.

A Picture

Alas, these are so easy to come by with the invention of Facebook and quality photography built into our cell phones. If you're forging a driver's license or some other piece of identification requiring a picture identification, to see how easy it is, just take a stroll through your friend's

Facebook photos. Look for head-on, high-resolution shots that could be used to forge an identity card. You'll be surprised.

A Credit Card or Banking Account Number

Obviously, it goes without saying, but if a hacker can access your money electronically, they can make purchases under your name, damage your credit, close and transfer account balances and apply for more credit. Facebook doesn't directly ask for this kind of information but consumers could be convinced to provide it in Facebook messaging or Facebook applications.

A Phone Number

Phone numbers are becoming increasingly important for account validation through text messaging. Undoing a restriction placed on a user account, an aggressor may need a telephone number to authorize an unlocking action. Further, telephone numbers are also becoming important in the context of *smishing* attacks – smishing is the act of sending text messages to convince them to do something through an emotional appeal, like, authorize a transaction or transfer money, when it's really a bogus attempt to have the cellular phone user authorize a charge against their phone bill.

Will There Ever be a Magic Pill?

In the software industry, over-promising is just part of the gig. Isn't it rather uncanny how the antivirus product you bought yesterday is touted as the most perfect security solution you could own, yet today your PC is still infected with *something*, and next year – when the next version is released – the vendor will convince you that it's as worthless as peanut-brittle.

Myself, I find that almost magical. Too magical. And by *magical* I mean *deceptive*.

Obviously, spending more money on upgrades isn't going to solve your problem. There will never be a magic pill that'll make you a 100-percent secure online and maintain absolute privacy. It won't be created by Facebook and Facebook should never promise it because it'd be a lie. Nobody can out-engineer nor out-spend human ingenuity and innovation. If you're a software developer, there's at least two dozen ways your product can be compromised that you haven't thought of, and others – in time – will gladly provide another two dozen more should you be suffering from a Hubris-inspired spell of self-delusion. Using the Internet in any capacity is risky. There's no quick fix from Facebook, Symantec, McAfee, Microsoft, or anybody else that will guarantee the privacy of our PPI while using our systems online.

Magical-thinking will get you in trouble. You'll spend a lot of money on solutions that'll never meet your expectations, that can't ever anticipate what it wasn't programed to understand, and you'll lose sight of the greatest risk that's in your power to address: yourself.

Minimizing Your Risks on Facebook

What You Will Learn

- The greatest risk to your privacy and security on Facebook is yourself
- Why changing your behavior is critical to your success
- Why your friends' behavior on Facebook puts you at risk
- How to create complex passwords
- How to use Facebook services to provide temporary login passwords
- How to think about your intentions on Facebook and why that's important
- Are you a *public*, *private*, or *guarded* figure on Facebook?

The Greatest Risk

Okay. So you might think the greatest risk to using Facebook are hackers bent on stealing your PPI or hordes of unscrupulous marketers who want to bug you at all hours of the day, or fraudsters who want to impersonate you for financial gain. Actually, these guys aren't the greatest risk to you. Not by a long shot.

The greatest risk to your privacy and security on Facebook is you. We've established your privacy and security depends heavily on your own behaviors and choices. What you do, what you say, and what you share.

What You Do

- Playing games on Facebook is a lot of fun but doing so reveals more information about you and grants Apps (Applications) access to your account. Remember, by default, when you play a game you're authorizing a third party to access your PPI and the PPI of your friends. The more games you play, the greater risk you have, and the greater exposure you present to your friends.

- Friend in others without knowing who they are – randomly granting access to your Facebook profile diminishes privacy. The more Facebook friends you acquire the greater risk you have.

- Connecting your Facebook information to other web sites – yep, that also diminishes privacy by surrendering PPI collected by Facebook to third parties – because it's convenient to automatically log in to the website using your Facebook credential. Here you've sacrificed confidentiality for convenience and the website operator expects that of you. The more websites you connect your Facebook Profile to the greater risk you have.

- Using the same password on Facebook as other web sites – a significant problem as your account could be easily compromised. The same password used across multiple websites greatly puts you at higher risk.

- The time that you spend online – why expect privacy when your actions are increasingly social? When what you say and do can be spread instantly, everywhere, at the speed of light? The more time you spend on Facebook reveals information about you, putting you at a greater loss of privacy.

- The security precautions you haven't taken – you may have taken no action to opt-out and protect your privacy. Inattention to opt-out settings in Facebook compromises your online privacy.

What You Say

- You intentionally provide incriminating information, facts, or details in your social content.

- Be mindful what you share with others – it can come back to haunt you; electronic content is never truly deleted.

- Stuff you say about others and your friends – facts, rumor, or speculation, it doesn't matter; what's said in an electronic space can still affect you in the real world.

- Aggressive behavior like bullying, cyber-stalking, or blackmail have real world ramifications.

- Information best addressed to a small, niche audience was published to a bunch of people, and then shared with a lot more people.

What You Share

- Slanderous, outrageous, vulgar, or inflammatory comments, photographs, or videos.

- Geolocation – data collected from your cell phone showing where you've been.

- If you share everything to everyone publically, then there's no expectation of privacy.

- If you share your Facebook password with others, or on other websites, then there's no expectation of security whatsoever.

The first step to consciously controlling your security and ensuring your privacy begins by controlling your behavior. It's awareness. *What you do, what you say, and what you share.* If you're completely oblivious to the consequences of uploading questionable content to Facebook, and saying outrageous things that are bound to spark controversy, well, no amount of software settings are going to help you. In such circumstances you've failed to even help yourself.

Creating an Effective Password

Certainly the second-most important thing you can do to preserve your privacy on Facebook is to set-up an effective complex password. Passwords are the only mechanism Facebook has to authenticate you and control access to your account. If your password is compromised, somebody can login as you and impersonate you, steal your PPI, misrepresent you to friends, family, or co-workers, or, resell your user credential to others for profit. Your password is the first and last line of defense in securing your time on Facebook.

Computer security experts like me talk about the need for complex passwords. Complex just means that you're creating passwords that are hard for a computer to guess. Variability in the password forces a computer to spend more time judging all of the random possibilities and that exponentially increases the time and risk expended by a hacker to crack it. Complex passwords force a standard microcomputer to spend many hundreds of years trying to crack your account, and a hacker would rather not wait that long – they're likely to spend time on the easy targets that haven't changed their behavior and use simple passwords because they're easier to hack. Thus a complex password is an effective deterrent. It's not perfect but it does dissuade a hacker from spending time on compromising your PPI. It encourages the hacker to go somewhere else instead of spend time on you.

How to Create a Complex Password

1. Pick two words. Try to make one related to a hobby or interest you have; make the second one a verb or an adjective.
2. Concatenate those words. Put them together.
3. Capitalize at least one character.
4. Replace letters with numbers. Make I's ones; O's zeros; E's threes.
5. Add a metacharacter at the end – examples: !#&(

Examples of complex passwords:

- g0lFsw1ng!
- (runW1ld)
- P0w3rb@ll!
- Ch33zypuff#
- P0pc0rnP0w3r
- Fluffyp01nt!

You've probably noticed that you can make sense of these words. Your mind can intuit the numbers as letters and substitution makes the password easier to remember. Meanwhile, computers will think these words are jibberish. It's not an equation, it's not a dictionary word, it's too random to guess at, and it's nonsense. Easy-peasy for humans; really tough for computers. That's what you want to think about.

One idea that I'd like you to take and implement right away: your Facebook password should be complex and it should be totally unlike anything you're already using online. It should be unique to Facebook and it shouldn't even vaguely resemble any of the 12 most valuable pieces of information we were just speaking about. This is something you could do right now that would go a long way in preserving your confidentiality on Facebook and in reducing your "attack profile" online.

Requesting a Temporary Password from Facebook

Are you concerned about using your Facebook password while on unfamiliar computers? You should be. Let's say you're traveling and would like to use a computer in a public library or hotel, or, a wireless network in an unsavory part of town. In your experience, you probably know that if you provide the password on this computer, it'll offer to store your credential permanently potentially allowing somebody to login to Facebook under your account. The wifi access point could be set-up to capture your passwords and login information because, well, it looks like free access to the Internet, and it's a common way to exploit naïve people. Yet, in a worst-case, a public computer could be compromised, hosting a virus or malware, just waiting to steal your Facebook credential. What you'd like to use right then and there is a temporary password that expires over time, and doesn't reveal your actual password to any computer system.

Facebook offers an often unknown process for using a temporary password to login to public computers. It's relatively simple to use:

1. Use a cell phone linked to your Facebook account.
2. On your cell phone, text "otp" to 32665.
3. You'll be texted back a temporary password that can only be used once and expires in 20 minutes.

Victims Don't Change Their Behaviors

Okay, you could look at using complex passwords or requesting a temporary password from Facebook as being super inconvenient. It's admittedly tricky to remember a password like this and then you'll probably expect me to say you should use different complex passwords everywhere, and of course you should! And even better, you should probably change your password to Facebook at least twice per year. Still, it's not terribly easy.

And that's the point. Humans are lazy. Humans don't want to be inconvenienced. The hacker is expecting you to be lazy and choose the most convenient option. They'll assume that you'll use the same password over and over again, and at multiple websites, because you're human. Predictable human behavior makes it easier for them and victims – regardless of risk - don't change their behaviors.

You see, the real benefit to using complex password is to force the hacker to go hack somebody else. Yep. You're creating an *opportunity cost* for the hacker by using them. Hackers are rational: they don't want to spend all of their scarce time trying to access your account. It's a lot easier to break into somebody else that doesn't use complex passwords and there are plenty of them. So the second step to protecting your Facebook presence is to stop being predictable. You've got to behave differently. Changing your behavior in favor of less convenience in exchange for tighter security will help you secure your time on Facebook.

Your Friend's Behavior Will Hurt You

On Facebook, your privacy is only as good as the behaviors practiced by your friends. If somebody in your Facebook network has a weak password and their Facebook Profile is hacked, they can send you malware and find out confidential information about you. 419, a common Facebook scam, is where a Facebook Profile is hacked and the hacker impersonates that user and sends a message to friends asking for money. And sooner or later, money is wired to Nigeria.[34]

So here's the third step. Friends on Facebook make you vulnerable. The inability of others to change their own behaviors – even when confronted with greater risk – will only hurt you. Inasmuch, there's a direct relationship: the more friends you have on Facebook, the greater potential for vulnerability. Limiting the number of friends you make on Facebook is yet another decision you can make to lower your attack profile.

You Are Your Own Enemy

I hope I've convinced you that Facebook security isn't strictly a technology problem but a human problem. It's a problem of accepting convenience over security, committing the same mistakes over and over again, expecting a different outcome, and it's a problem of scale. There are millions upon millions of users on Facebook whose interconnectedness makes everyone exponentially vulnerable. You are your own worst enemy. But hey, don't freak out. It's not all doom and gloom. Facebook can be a fun place. It can also be made reasonably secure provided you're willing to take a few reasonable precautions to reduce your own vulnerability. You can choose to do something about the risks we've discussed so far or – like many others – you can choose to ignore it, yet so much of our security on Facebook and the confidentiality of our PPI depends on our willingness to adapt to risk. What are you going to do about it? How will you adapt? What actions are you going to take now? Well, that may entirely depend upon your intentions on Facebook, and that's the fourth security idea that

I'd like to share with you.

What's My Intention on Facebook?

If I haven't given you pause to at least consider the risks involved with social networking then my arguments presented thus far must be falling on deaf ears. If you're at all concerned about risk and want to do something about it, you'll want to think clearly about how and why you're going to use Facebook.

- Will it be to connect with my immediate friends and family?

- Will it be to connect to – additionally or exclusively – coworkers, vendors, or customers?

- Will it be to build an audience for self-branding and marketing, or, will you be a social spectator?

- Will it be to play games and interact with your closest friends?

- Will it be to interact with brands, ideas, and people all around the world, or, a niche of people?

- Will Facebook become a hub for authorizing your access to other websites?

I'll use myself as an example.

I use Facebook much like everyone else: as a means to connect with my friends and family. However, I also use it to connect to students, customers, vendors, service providers, and readers. I use Facebook as a means to promote my products, my company, my books, and my services. I want to deliberately spread what I do, say, and share around because more visibility equals a potential connection, and more connections may lead to greater revenue opportunity. The more content I create, the more content I want scanned and available to search engines, and I want to be easily found everywhere. This means that I'm a *public figure* on Facebook.

Now let's consider Mrs. Betsy Sharp, a fictional 58-year-old mother of three who uses Facebook to keep up with her grandkids and extended family. Mrs. Sharp is a person that follows only a select number of people on Facebook. Her interactions are probably conducted in a narrowband – that's to say she shares content with a very small group of friends. She isn't an extraordinarily outspoken person and she doesn't spend a lot of time on Facebook playing games, engaging in discussions, reading posts or status updates, or looking at pictures. She doesn't understand how multiple websites can use her Facebook profile for single-sign-on and she doesn't care about the benefits of personalization offered by a single-sign-on. Facebook is used almost like email to Betsy. In this case, Mrs. Sharp is a *private figure* on Facebook.

Finally, let's consider another fictional party, Tim Johnson, a 38-year-old business owner who uses Facebook as a community outreach and sales tool.

Tim is a gregarious and outspoken individual who loves to use Facebook as a way to communicate to everybody. He uploads photos, pictures, provides regular status updates every hour, and engages in complex conversations online. He simplifies his access to other websites by engaging single-sign-on – allowing Facebook to authorize him to everywhere he goes on the web – because he finds this convenient and fast, and he likes the personalization. Yet, Tim is smart enough to know he needs to conceal specific pieces of information about him. He's a visible business owner and a target for identity theft. Tim also needs to target what he says to specific audiences. He needs to strike a balance between being a public persona yet safeguard his PPI. Tim is a *guarded figure* on Facebook.

Think about it: are you a *public*, *private*, or *guarded figure* on Facebook? Understanding your intention will help clarify some of the software settings that we're about to discuss, and it'll define the kinds of audiences you'll build within your social network.

So, if you're concerned about Facebook privacy, I'd first try to have you think about these five broad ideas:

1. Risk
2. Awareness
3. Passwords
4. Friends
5. Intent

It's from here that we can have a more thorough discussion about Facebook's settings to secure your account to a level of risk and exposure that you're comfortable with. Let's get started.

How to Secure Your Facebook Account

What You Will Learn

- What is the default privacy and security position of every user on Facebook
- An explanation of Facebook's account security settings
- Recommendations for every setting
- How to use Facebook Mobile to introduce another factor for authentication

Facebook's Default Privacy and Security Settings

The designers of Facebook believe that your intention is to be as *public* a figure as possible, and by default, the following sharing and security options are bestowed upon new Facebook users:

- Secure browsing is disabled. The material you send to Facebook across the web is not encrypted.

- Login notifications are disabled. Multiple logins under your account can take place and you're not notified.

- Login approvals are disabled. Any login event from any device is authorized.

- Security questions are not set. They must be manually set by the user.

- Everything you post in status updates are in the public domain – everyone and every application on Facebook can scan, read, search for, and digest the updates, photos, and videos you post.

- Everything you've ever posted in the past is in the public domain.

- Everyone can find you and send you friend requests and send you a message.

- Any of your friends can write on your wall.

- Friends of your friends can see posts left by others on your wall.

- Photos that are uploaded by friends get a facial recognition process ran over them. Faces of your friends are tagged, and friends of your friends can see those tags.

- Your friends can check you in to physical places using mobile devices.

- When using apps, games, and websites, over 20 separate pieces of your PPI on Facebook are selected 'on' and sharable by default.

- Instant personalization features are enabled so that PPI can be shared with third parties and single-sign-on can be performed.

- Users can be personally searched for within Facebook.

- Your address and phone number are exposed to your friends within Facebook.

- All of the following PPI identified within the user's profile is exposed to the public domain:

    - Hometown
    - Current City
    - Sexual preference, relationship statuses, family relationships, and friends
    - Languages spoken
    - About me narrative
    - Education and work background
    - Favorite quotations and inspirational figures
    - All arts and entertainment, sports, and activities and interests selections
    - Your website

Pretty wide open, huh?

As we've discussed, Facebook practices a security philosophy of *default opt-in*. Facebook leans towards settings that maximize sharing and minimize inconvenience. Again, more restrictive security settings would run contrary to their function. If we're at all concerned about privacy, we must respond accordingly.

And so the question becomes: what rational steps can we take within Facebook to reasonably protect the confidentiality surrounding our PPI, and, give us greater confidence securing our privacy? What settings can we toggle in Facebook to assert greater control over our privacy? Each of these settings will be discussed in the context of *intention* – from the perspective of the *public* figure, the *private* figure, and the *guarded* figure. Facebook Account Settings are found by down-selecting the arrow on the upper-right of the screen aside the word HOME next to your name. All of the subsequent settings are found in the screens encountered thereafter.

General Security Settings

Facebook > Account Settings > General > Name

Using this setting, you can change your first, middle, and last name recorded with Facebook. In order to make the change, you'll need your account password. How does Facebook know who you really are in the first place? They honest answer is they don't. They don't call you, check-up on you, or lookup your Social Security Number. Facebook simply relates a person to an email address. If you have multiple email addresses, it's feasible to have multiple Facebook accounts.

Now before you go-gonzo here and start creating multiple fake Facebook accounts, you should know doing so is against their Terms and Conditions. Facebook will remove fake accounts if they find them. Further, Facebook has become pretty adept at discovering suspicious behavior where the same computer is using their system over and over with multiple accounts; you should understand that's easy to catch with simple technical controls. There's also a means for users to report fake accounts to Facebook. Facebook would like every person to own just one Facebook account. One account, one person, on Facebook.

Public, Private, Guarded: I recommend that you do not provide your middle name – you'll find that it's optional.

Private: Provide a nickname, what Facebook calls an Alternate Name. You will find a configurable option for this on the same screen. It will help mask your true identity with an alias. I certainly wouldn't recommend a maiden name as Facebook suggests in their help documentation.

Facebook > Account Settings > General > Username

On Facebook, a "username" is actually a customized Universal Resource
Locator (URL) that points directly to your profile on Facebook; mine, for
example, is russell.mickler, so if somebody wanted to find me on
Facebook, they'd enter http://www.facebook.com/russell.mickler into
their web browser. That'd pull me right up on Facebook, lickidy-split. This
tool allows you to reserve your own username and assign it to your profile,
provided that it hasn't already been reserved by someone else.

Public: Listen, if you're a Public figure on Facebook, a custom URL is
essential to your personal brand. You want to make it very easy for people
to find you! You will want to officially reserve your little slice of Facebook
for yourself right away.

Private and Guarded: On the other hand, there's security through
obscurity! Usually, Facebook's default URL to a profile is a very long set of
numbers and alphabetic characters. It's impossible to remember, and it's
not obviously related to your account. Don't touch this option if you want to
remain anonymous on Facebook.

Facebook > Account Settings > General > Email

Facebook understands two classifications of email accounts on their
system: primary and alternates. A primary email account is the one you
use to login to Facebook and it's linked to your profile. All of the others you
might provide are a way of Facebook to recognize who you are and they're
considered alternates.

Why more alternates? When people join Facebook, they're asked if

Facebook can rummage through their address book to find potential matches of email addresses to profiles. The more email addresses Facebook knows of you, then the easier it is to potentially link you to somebody else. More alternate email addresses makes Facebook's life a lot easier to match you to potential friends.

Public: You will want to use your public-facing email address representing your brand, company, or products. You want to associate those ideas to you and email is an easy way to accomplish this. Then, load-up as many alternate email addresses as you feel is appropriate. The easier it is for people to connect to you, the more friends you're likely to acquire when they sign-up for Facebook.

Guarded: You can hide and obscure your email address through Facebook. You can limit its exposure to a List of your choice, or, hide it entirely within your profile's privacy settings. Generally, it's okay to provide your trusted (principal) email account here – after all, you're networking, and you'll want to make it easy for close friends and family on Facebook to contact you – but don't make it super-easy. Provide only your trusted email address and don't provide any alternates.

Private: You may be suspicious of Facebook's behavior. You may not want to hand-over your trusted email account, and you may not want to be easily found on Facebook. Instead of using your trusted email address, use an untrusted one; for a description of trusted and untrusted email addresses, read my COP Methods section towards the end of the book. That way, Facebook or its 3rd party partners really won't know your real, principal email address.

Facebook > Account Settings > General > Password

Public, Guarded, Private: Now's your change to provide a complex password. You'll need your current password, of course, to authorize a new password. Take this option seriously. Provide a complex password and rotate it at least twice a year. You'll also notice that Facebook conveniently tells you how long it's been since the last time you rotated your password.

Facebook > Account Settings > General > Linked Accounts

In Facebook's understanding of this idea, a Linked Account is a Single-Sign-On (SSO) process where you pass your username and password from another system (like Google's Gmail, Yahoo! Mail, MSN, and others) and that successful login can confirm your Facebook identity. Conceivably, it makes it easier for you to access Facebook by remembering a single set of credentials. How convenient!

Public, Guarded, Private: Unfortunately, enabling any kind of SSO puts your Facebook account at significant risk. You'll recall our discussion on *convenience*. If somebody hacks your Gmail account, they suddenly have access to your Facebook account, too. Why would you ever want to do that? Regardless of your intention on Facebook, it's probably a better idea to steer-clear of this option and leave it turned off. I wouldn't recommend you link any account you might have to Facebook.

Facebook > Account Settings > Language

Public, Guarded, Private: This setting conveys your primary language to Facebook. It's a required setting but it can be changed. This language setting - unlike the Languages section in your timeline/profile – is a real language and is used to localize Facebook to your preferences.

Downloading a Copy of Your Facebook Data (Account Settings)

Public, Guarded, Private: Facebook offers a means of extracting your PPI from Facebook in the form of a crude backup. It has two modes: a regular mode and an enhanced mode. Processing this option essentially allows you to take a snapshot of your Facebook presence and pull it down to your computer. It's a backup. However, it's not a very useful backup. You could not, for example, use this archive to re-upload into Facebook to restore missing information. It's just a one-day shot to get at your PPI and put it on your PC. You'd use this option if you were looking to make a copy of your Facebook data for the long term.

Facebook > Account Settings > Security > Security Question

Public, Guarded, Private: Security questions are a means to challenge a user and prove ownership of their Facebook account. Facebook provides the question and you provide an answer, and you'll need to confirm the change. We should all have good security questions. Make it something you can remember rather than writing it down. Remembering the answer to this question adds just a bit more security.

Facebook > Account Settings > Security > Secure Browsing

When an Internet browser browses the web it normally works in a state called 'plaintext'. That's to say that everything it transmits on the Internet is unencrypted and can be seen by anyone who happens to be watching. That's really risky. Securing the browser connection forces it into another state called 'Secure Sockets Layer' (SSL) and it encrypts the activities in the browser between the client machine and the Facebook server. You'll see your browser enter SSL whenever it prefixes the URL with https:// and a lock appears.

Public, Guarded, Private: Whatever your intention might be on Facebook, it's a great practice to secure everything you do online behind encryption. That's just a practical piece of advice. Enable this feature right away.

Facebook > Account Settings > Security > Login Notifications

As we get around to it in this book, you'll learn that Facebook can keep track of the computers and devices that you usually log in to Facebook with. Facebook can therefore be setup to notify you through email or text messaging that a login under your account took place on a PC or device that wasn't previously authorized.

Public: First, I'll preface what I'm about to say with a common-sense approach. You should turn this feature on, at least the email portion. But let me give you my advice learned from the school of hard-knocks. If you're a public figure who travels frequently, or performs public speaking that involves logging in to Facebook on podiums and random computers, you're going to get deluged with notices. Consider how frequently you use different devices and choose appropriately.

Guarded and Private: You'll want to enable this feature, at least the email portion; for the Private-intended person, enable the text messaging to your mobile device. If somebody attempts to compromise your Facebook account, you'll be immediately made aware of the activity and could take some swift corrective action.

Facebook > Account Settings > Security > Login Approvals

In the security field, we play around with ideas that are related to factors of authentication. There are three common factors: what you know, what you have, and who you are.

When you're challenged for a password to Facebook, this is a single-factor form of authentication. You provide what you know and you get in. However, a single-factor form of authentication is relatively weak as compared to a dual-factor like your ATM card. To access your bank account, you need the card with a mag-stripe, and, a PIN: something you have and something you know; even better if it had a third, like, a required biometric scan of your thumbprint. Regardless, two or three factors are a lot better than one!

What this option does is create a two-factor form of authentication for Facebook. Facebook presumes that you've got a password, but now, every time there's a login of your account to an unauthorized device, Facebook will text your cell phone – something you have – with a unique six-digit code. That code will be necessary to complete the login and authorize the new device.

Public, Guarded, Private: I personally believe this is a great feature for the security-minded person and you should enable it, but it's a bit of an over-kill if you're constantly logging-in to new devices. This is a great feature for anyone who is always logging-in to Facebook on the same stuff (PC's, phones, laptops, and tablet computers). Every new device will generate a text confirmation and these can get annoying after a while. In fact, you'll be inundated with text confirmations the moment you start signing in to every device you own. Try out this feature though. If somebody tries to compromise your account, you'll be notified and they won't have the secret code because they won't have your cell phone. Well, you hope. Don't lose your cell-phone. If you do, jump into the Mobile Settings and click on the "lose your phone?" link to de-register your authorized mobile device and register a new one right away.

Facebook > Account Settings > Security > App Passwords

What if you didn't feel right about handing over your Facebook password to every website that wanted to connect to your Facebook account? What if you wanted to generate a unique password for every app to access your FB account, and control the revocation of access at your own leisure?

Public, Guarded, Private: If you're as paranoid as I am, of course you feel this way! And if you're a public figure on Facebook, you very much want to enable this feature and have Facebook generate a unique password for apps that access information across the Internet. Now, this feature is a bit crude – it currently requires you to know the name of the app you wish to assign a password to instead of selecting it from a list. Still, a great feature to protect your account's actual password and to pass an application-specific password to your account that you can control.

Facebook > Account Settings > Security > Recognized Devices

Recognized devices on Facebook are your phones, tablets, laptops, and PC's that you've used to access Facebook and have authorized for your use. If you've enabled Login Approvals, you're going to see all of the devices that you've authorized over time.

Public: Enable this feature. Keep in mind: as a public person on Facebook, you're a target. Some caution should be exercised by periodically deleting all of the devices that you don't immediately recognize. If you're done speaking at a particular school, delete the lectern computer from your approved devices right away; if you've moved-on to a new mobile phone, delete your old one; if you logged in to a friend's tablet to show them some cool new feature, delete the tablet's approval. Take the time to manage your approved devices and limit the number of actual devices that are currently in use – doing so will reduce your attack profile.

Guarded: Enable this feature. If you don't recognize a device, there's no harm in removing it. You can always re-authorize it later if necessary. *Private:* Enable this feature and take no chances. Delete any device that you aren't consciously aware of, and afterwards, rotate your account password. Limit the number of devices you use.

Facebook > Account Settings > Security > Active Sessions

Uh-oh. Traveled to your mom's house last weekend and you're uncertain if you logged-off of Facebook from her computer? Have no fear: Active Sessions Manager is here.

Public, Guarded, Private: This is actually a pretty cool security feature of Facebook albeit very geeky. It shows all of the "active" sessions that devices have had using your account. It shows you the time, date, and device name, the duration of the session, and an approximated geography. Typically, you will find active sessions with approved devices still "active" from a couple of days to several months. There could be lots of active sessions and many of them you might not be using. If any session has expired and you're not using it, just hit the End Activity button. That will cancel the security token and force the user to re-authenticate and generate a new one.

Now, if you don't recognize an approved device in this list, or, there's somebody from Scotland logged in as you – and you're quite confident you haven't been traveling through Scotland recently – now's the time to End Activity on that session and rotate your password right away. Nobody from Scotland should be using your account! With Active Sessions Manager, you can remotely log them off. That forcibly disconnects the session and will require the user to log back in. Make sure to follow that up by rotating your password, maybe deleting any Apps you don't recognize, and report the incident to Facebook.

Facebook > Account Settings > Notifications

Facebook Notifications are announcements generated from Facebook to notify you of certain events, like, somebody posts to your wall, or, somebody leaves you a message, talks about you, or tags you. Whatever. Facebook operates in a very promiscuous mode: it wants to notify you of everything that it can so it can shoot you emails and text messages to pull you back into the site. In this section, you can see notifications that were made today and your notification settings.

Public, Guarded, Private: When I think about Facebook Notifications, I think about being constantly annoyed whenever somebody happens to interact with me on Facebook. Very shortly, my email inbox becomes swamped with Facebook notifications. In general, I'd advocate you turn off notifications in Facebook by editing each section, with some noteworthy exceptions:

1. *Facebook > Account Settings > Notifications > Email Frequency.* Turn this off to allow you to toggle individual notification settings.

2. *Facebook > Sends You a Message*. Leave this notification on. A message is a form of direct correspondence in Facebook. You'd want visibility over messages.

3. *Facebook > Mentions You in a Comment*. Leave this notification on. If somebody directly tags you in a status update or comment, you can receive an announcement that you were mentioned and follow-up on the conversation.

4. *Photos > Tags You in a Photo*. Leave this notification on. If somebody (or Facebook) tags you in a photograph that has been uploaded, you'd probably like the opportunity to inspect it.

5. *Events > Invites You to an Event*. Leave this notification on. If somebody invites you to an event on Facebook, you would want to be notified.

6. *Video > Tags You in a Video*. Leave this notification on. If somebody (or Facebook) tags you in a video that's been uploaded, you'd want the opportunity to inspect it.

7. *Other Updates from Facebook > Updates About Reports You Filed*. Leave this notification on. If you end up using the features at Facebook to report fraud and abuse, you'd want email notifications to let you know pending statuses on those cases.

Facebook Mobile Settings

The history of Facebook is deeply rooted with mobile phones. So much so that Facebook has a specific set of security controls surrounding mobile devices and text messaging. You can access it at www.facebook.com/mobile but those settings can also be edited from within Facebook's Account Settings page.

There are several advantages to setting up a mobile device on Facebook, the least of which is that setup creates an authorized device through which to receive Logon Approvals. You can also download the latest Facebook App for your smartphone from the Mobile site.

Facebook > Account Settings > Mobile

Public, Guarded, or Private: I would recommend enabling the text messaging feature as to take advantage of other security features found in Facebook. Register just one phone and de-register (remove) phones that are lost or stolen.

You can be notified when various events take place in Facebook by a text message. Turning text notifications on or off is a matter of preference, but if your intention is to be a Private person on Facebook, you'd probably want to turn all notifications off or delineate hours for text messaging to control the annoyance factor. If you'd like to keep the text notification option on but de-select notifications for commenting and friend notifications, you can do that here.

Also, if you're a person with a metered text messaging package on their phone, you probably want to turn most of these notifications off or set a daily text limit to prevent Facebook from burning through your text plan.

Facebook > Account Settings > Payments

Facebook Credits are an electronic currency used to buy things within Facebook games. You pay real money with a credit card, mobile phone, or Paypal to purchase credits. Within this section, you can setup Payment

Methods, examine your Payment History, set a Preferred Currency for each transaction, and even setup Subscriptions to automatically renew your payments balance with Facebook.

Public, Guarded, or Private: Payments are only necessary if you're going to be playing games on Facebook that require credits. It is not necessary to provide any information in this section of Facebook if that's not your intention. If you are going to be playing such games, try using a credit card or Paypal account that isolates Facebook from your regular checking account; see my COP methods at the end of the book.

Facebook > Account Settings > Facebook Ads > Ads Shown by Third Parties

Social plugins are easy-to-use code snipits that link a third-party website to Facebook. Maybe you've seen them? You browse to a website and see a Facebook-colored box where three or six faces from Facebook users who have "liked" a Facebook Page are presented. You may question whether or not you'd like your smiling mug presented on a website operated by a third-party to Facebook.

By default, Facebook does not give third party applications the right to use your name or your profile picture in advertisements, yet it would seem that they offer this setting just in case they "allow this in the future", and even the setting seems to suggest that it'll only be relevant "If we allow this in the future".

Public, Guarded, or Private: It's an interesting setting because Facebook seems to be suggesting that they will – at some point – start allowing third party applications the ability to use your name or picture in advertising.

They don't do it now ... but they might. Well, okay. In my opinion,
regardless if you're a Private, Guarded, or Public person on Facebook, you
should just as well set this option to "No One".

Facebook > Account Settings > Facebook Ads > Ads and Friends

Facebook believes that you want to share your social activities with
advertisers and that your Facebook friends wants to receive advertising
messages related to those activities. If you're using Facebook and end up
"liking" an advertisement, the ad will notify your Friends that you "like" the
advertisement. This is a social proof: an affirmation that encourages your
friends to also like the advertisement which, in turn, directs them to a
Facebook Page or third party website.

Public, Guarded, or Private: In my opinion, a thumbs-up from me next to a
piece of advertising appears as an endorsement of a product or service,
and that may not be the message I'm comfortable sending out into the
public domain. Regardless if you're a Private, Guarded, or Public person
on Facebook, I'd recommend that you set this option to "No One".

How to Use Facebook Lists

What You Will Learn

- How Lists on Facebook are used as native content filters
- How Lists can be used to target content to specific audiences
- How Lists are a part of Facebook's security model
- How Lists are used to screen content as a security mechanism and maintain confidentiality

Facebook Lists

The next concept we should explore when understanding how to control our privacy on Facebook are list. Lists work like filters in Facebook. Facebook users are able to create customized lists of friends, family, co-workers, customers, vendors, college buddies, or just about anybody. Content that's uploaded to Facebook can target a specific list. Lists can be found in the left-hand navigation element on Facebook, mid-way down the screen. Depending on your screen's resolution, you may need to press [more] then hover your mouse over the Lists section to see another [more] option … which will then allow you to edit your lists.

Lists represent a target audience. Users on Facebook can upload and post content intended for a specific audience while excluding content from all others. Lists also allow Facebook users to reduce the noise in their news stream so they can focus on updates provide by a single audience. Facebook has kindly pre-populated lists for you based on your family, work, and education associations. There should be lists for the schools and universities that you've attended, lists for your close friends and acquaintances, your family, and for the companies you've worked for. You can merge and combine some of these lists, delete them, and create new lists for your own purposes, although Facebook won't allow you to delete some lists that it created for you. Facebook uses those lists for security functions.

A Circle of Trust

Public, Guarded, or Private: I would highly recommend you create a list called Circle of Trust. If you're like me, you've a very select number of people who know a lot about you and you probably wouldn't mind sharing a lot of intimate details concerning your life with them. Your Circle of Trust could be contrasted against the whole of your family or friends who might be a little more than acquaintances and with anybody whom you may have some hesitation about sharing such intimate details with.

Your Circle of Trust is a very selective audience and a closed channel. You're likely to communicate almost anything within your Circle of Trust whereas other lists may be used to post content to different audiences – like co-workers, family, customers, and the like. Create as many audiences (lists) as you feel you need but don't create too many of them or you'll spend your waking hours trying to manage their composition, and that's no fun. Social networking shouldn't be all about maintaining filters.

Once lists are created, you'll find that they can now be used to target posts, status updates, notes, videos, pictures, and profile content. Almost anything you share on Facebook can be geared towards a specific list – a specific audience – that you define. Unless you change the default privacy setting, Facebook will always post content to a public domain, meaning that anyone anywhere on Facebook can read, use, and access that material. When you hear horror stories of where people have posted compromising information that became accessible to future employers, co-workers, or even somebody's parents or grandmother, it's because they posted it to the public domain. Through audience targeting through lists, you're able to direct your content to a much narrower audience and conceal those posts from those who're not a part of your list. They're not part of your Circle of Trust.

Through the practice of using lists and deliberately releasing content to specific audiences, you can change your behavior as to direct information only to approved parties. It may be a little tough to do the advanced planning, to think about these lists and to manage them over time, but their benefit is clear: we can separate the questionable content on Facebook from what we share in the public domain.

How to Secure Your Facebook Profile

What You Will Learn

- What the difference is between a Facebook Profile and a Facebook Page
- The settings on Facebook to secure your Facebook Profile
- Recommendations for use

Profiles and Pages

On Facebook, a Profile is the information associated with a regular person while a Page is information associated with a topic, cause, a celebrity, a business or non-profit, a book, community, school, even silly ideas ... anything you might consider a non-person or celebrity can be a Page.

Facebook users set up Pages. They can setup and administer as many Pages as they want. Pages are a way to create another channel on Facebook to divide an audience.

Pages are inherently a very public thing on Facebook and they follow some very specific rules.

First off, Pages can't "friend" anybody - they must to be "liked" by an active user on Facebook. That means some user on Facebook encounters the Page and "likes" it which is the same as saying that they've "subscribed" to the Page and wish to receive content from it. Users can also unsubscribe or "unlike" a Page should they find the content disagreeable. Per Facebook's Terms and Conditions, businesses and other non-people must be Pages and not regular user accounts with Profiles. That rule prevents Facebook from becoming a huge spamming playground. Pages can be voluntarily subscribed to and unsubscribed from.

Second, unlike user Profiles, everything posted on a Page is posted to the public domain. Content posted to a Page is available to search engines and accessible by all on Facebook. You can't target or filter content based off of lists because lists are only tools available to Facebook users.

Third, interactions that take place between Pages and active users on Facebook are logged and tracked. A built-in statistical analysis tool called Facebook Insights allows people who own Pages to examine how effective their social media marketing strategy is. Only Pages can track this information within Facebook; Profiles do not track this information.

Channeling Your Audience

If you're a private person on Facebook, you likely have no business creating and using Facebook Pages. Socially on Facebook, you're an introvert or at best a social spectator and you're not actively publishing content to a public audience. Hey, that's okay - no harm no foul - but you don't need to know about Pages.

However, if you're a public or guarded person on Facebook, you might look at Pages as a way to build relationships under a single branded Page, cultivate that audience, co-manage that content, isolate its relationships to that Page instead of your own Profile – maintaining some degree of separation between who you might consider "friends" on Facebook over people just following your ideas – and measure your performance. It'd be a much more effective way to create a public channel for content than lists and the Page has more tools available to your marketing efforts.

Public or Guarded: This is when you might consider building and using Pages to help channel your audience. The strategy would be to encourage others to "like" your Page and to channel all of your communication to them across the Page. Through using Pages, you'd be using the native features of Facebook to create, develop, and cultivate a fan base for your own nefarious purposes: your business, your book, your pet projects, your political ideas, social experiments, or brands. And naturally, Facebook would highly encourage this because they love public, searchable content, and they created Pages specifically for this purpose.

Securing Your Facebook Profile

Facebook users have all of their PPI stored under Profiles. Recently, Facebook has offered users the option to "upgrade" from Profiles to Timelines and event more recently Facebook converted all Profiles to Timelines. Thank you, Facebook: until that happened, it required me to list the two potential options in my settings discussion. Now it's not necessary. Every Facebook user can take direct steps to secure their profile by changing the privacy settings in their Timeline, but before you begin changing your Timeline, I would recommend that you set up your Circle of Trust list. You'll need this list before you can assign filters and Profile permissions. Thereafter, you can edit your Timeline by logging in to Facebook, clicking on your name and face found in the upper-right bar, and by clicking on the Update Info button.

Remember that the Facebook Timeline is a tool that Facebook uses to relate ideas, concepts, brands, entertainment, activities and interests directly to you as a person. Also remember that Facebook tries to set all of this information to a public domain status because doing so primarily benefits them, and, Facebook assumes that you want to be as public a person as possible on their network. Taking steps to secure your Timeline and ratchet-up the privacy settings is a means of restricting access to approved Facebook users in lists and denying access to all others (applications, Facebook users, and third parties) who're not a part of those lists.

Aside nearly every entry in your Facebook Profile is a drop-down selector that allows you to set who can see the subject information in your Profile, and there are six generalized settings:

Public: If the item in your Profile is set to Public, this information is available to anyone and everyone on Facebook, including third-parties to Facebook. It is the least restrictive setting.

Friends: If the item in your Profile is set to Friends, then this information is only available to people who have "friended" you on Facebook. Direct access by third-parties is excluded, although third-parties who access your information from permission granted to them by your friends is still applicable. This means that your Facebook friends can allow others to access your information through them which is particularly concerning.

Friends of Friends: If a friend of your friend on Facebook tries to see your Profile, they will have access to see this information. Direct access by third-parties is again excluded, but still, friends can allow access to your information through their own settings.

Only Me: The most restrictive setting, this instructs Facebook not to display this information to anyone.

Lists: You can limit content to a specific audience by choosing a list. If you created that Circle of Trust list that I mentioned earlier, any piece of information that you flag to the Circle of Trust is only viewable by them, and is excluded from others and third parties.

Custom: The most specific setting, you can identify a particular set of users who can have direct access to a piece of information found on your Profile. And after changing the setting in your Profile, make sure to hit the Save Changes button found at the bottom of the page. That will put your new settings into motion.

Facebook > Timeline > Update Info > Living

Facebook and its partners can tell a lot about you by understanding where you live and where you grew up. That helps target marketing and advertising towards you, include you on searches, and re-confirm your potential identity. Further, city information can be used by people who want to commit identity theft.

Public: If your intention is to be as public as possible on Facebook, you would want to leave these settings as Public. You want to make it as easy as possible for anyone to find you and not confuse you with others on Facebook.

Guarded: If you wish to take a Guarded stance, set both your Hometown and Current City to your Circle of Trust.

Private: Don't make it easy for Facebook to presume who you are or to provide its partners with your marketing information. Lock this down! Set both your Hometown and Current City to *Only Me.*

Facebook > Timeline > Update Info > Basic Info > I Am

Social networks are very interested in your gender and you'll notice that Facebook doesn't offer an opt-out on this piece of information. It's automatically public and can be accessed by third-parties. However, you can restrict if active Facebook users actually see your gender on your Profile by de-selecting "Show my sex in my profile". Keep in mind: although this prevents users from seeing this information, it's still accessible by third-parties.

Facebook > Timeline > Update Info > Basic Info > Birthday

One of the twelve most important things about you, your birthday is a particularly valuable piece of information to Facebook, and you'll notice that there's no way to actually limit how this information is used. That's because Facebook and its third-party associates want to be able to calculate your current age for marketing and advertising purposes, and it's essential that Facebook offer that information to them. Facebook also provides friendly event announcements to your friends to remind them that it's your birthday. And your birthday can be exported into your friend's calendars and other programs. Birthdays are critical to Facebook and, again, they don't offer a way to completely turn this information off.

Public: Still, if your intention is to be a public person on Facebook, I'd recommend that you enter your Birthday and select the option "Don't show my birthday in my profile". This prevents active Facebook users from actually seeing the birthday but won't prevent applications and third-parties from actually using it to help confirm who you are.

Guarded and Private: Regardless of the option to conceal your birthday, does the idea that others can access your birthday on Facebook still give you the heebie-jeebies? Yeah, I don't blame you. What if you entered a fake birthday instead and flipped this setting to "Don't show in my profile"? Sure, those friendly event reminders would be inaccurate, but at least your real birthday wouldn't be made available to others.

Facebook > Timeline > Update Info > Basic Info > Interested In

Social networks being as they are, Facebook understands that there might be others interested in pursuing a romantic relationship with you and Facebook uses this setting as a social signal for your sexual orientation. It can also be a way to advertise to you through third-parties.

Public: Do as you will, and leave the privacy setting as Public.

Guarded: I recommend you limit this setting to your Circle of Trust. Really, only your close friends should know your sexual orientation anyway.

Private: First, uncheck either option. Just leave them both blank – keep them guessing. Second, I recommend you limit this setting to Only Me. Nobody but you should have to know this information anyway.

Facebook > Timeline > Update Info > Basic Info > Languages

Interestingly enough, this Language setting has nothing to do with the way that Facebook presents itself to you or "localizes" information. It's just a way to direct specific kinds of advertising and content to you. The Languages that are presented in this list aren't exactly real anyway - start typing the language and a list of available choices will appear. Try Klingon, Middle English, or Vulgar Latin on for size. Obviously this information can be populated for fun or even just left blank.

Public: Enter the languages you speak and leave this setting Public. It allows all Facebook users and its third-parties to know how to address you.

Guarded: Enter the languages you speak and assign the privacy setting to Circle of Trust. Facebook itself gets to know how to address you and how to provide content to you, but this information gets concealed from active Facebook users and third-parties; only those within your Circle of Trust can view it.

Private: Enter the languages you speak and limit this setting to Only Me. Otherwise, if you feel nobody else really needs to know this, delete the languages. Just leave it blank and set it to Only Me.

Facebook > Timeline > Update Info > About You > About Me

Public: Go ahead! Be very descriptive. Provide a paragraph or two about yourself and leave this setting as Public. Make sure to include some keywords and search terms that relate to your personal brand, product, or service.

Guarded: You may not wish to be as generous with personal information in this About Me narrative, and you may wish to set this information to your Circle of Trust.

Private: Provide little or nothing at all then set this information to Only Me.

Facebook > Timeline > Select Facebook Photo

I mentioned earlier that Facebook is built around people and unquestionably what makes a person a 'person' in Facebook is their Profile Picture. Your Facebook picture is an opportunity to relate your personality to others on the social network, causes you may wish to be directly associated with, and many people spend a lot of time thinking about their picture.

Your picture can also be associated to the Pages and brands that you like on Facebook, and your picture can be used in a variety of ways that you might otherwise not want to see – like, for example, your Facebook picture scattered across the Internet in social plug-ins, finding your photo related to a cause you'd otherwise not want everyone to know you support, or used within a Facebook game. This may bring you pause.
What will really bring you pause, however, is the fact that Facebook uses a form of facial recognition to identify you when you upload this picture, and then attempts to find and tag you when your friends upload other photos of you. Yikes!

Facebook has very few rules concerning the use of photos for Profile pictures. They must be devoid of nudity, refrain from suggestive or sexual acts, no body parts – these are faces - and be relatively family friendly. Other than that, they don't seem to have any published guidelines. Here are some of my ideas.

Public: If you're a public figure on Facebook, you want a clear and non-obscured headshot with you smiling, close-up and not from a distance, with excellent lighting. You are friendly and inviting. You are social. This picture includes only you – your spouse and kids aren't in this photo. There is a one-to-one relationship between the profile and the person depicted in the photo. This is the cleanest way to express who you are to Facebook.

Guarded: Use a photo editing software to convert your photo into a graphic image depicting you as a caricature. This is a likeness where people can obviously relate to you yet your image can't be easily recognized by software. You may opt to include your spouse or kids in this photo, making it harder for the facial recognition process to do its work (the computer must ponder which face it 'sees' is really yours, if what it 'sees' is really a face at all).

Private: Use a photo caricature that heavily distorts your likeness, or, provide an image that conceals a third of your face through darkness or is simply cropped. In this way, software cannot complete the facial recognition process. I would recommend that you provide some photo for a Profile picture, however. Facebook is a book of faces and faces are people; if you're going to be social, you should be uploading a picture.

Facebook > Timeline > Update Info > Relationship and Family

One of the coolest features in Facebook is the ability to draw a line from your Profile to the Profile of others on Facebook with whom you share a real-life relationship. Yet this is also one of the most privacy-challenged features in that Facebook (and its third-party partners) can programmatically step through those relationships and relate content back to you.

Imagine the amazing marketing potential! Este Lauder, for example, could personally remind me about my anniversary and suggest a compelling gift for my wife using her first name; it could be a rather good recommendation, too, since Este Lauder may even relate purchasing experiences back to my wife and understand some of her previous buying behaviors. How convenient!

However, now imagine the amazing privacy problems. Somebody could easily draw a line from my wife to her father, immediately seizing upon her maiden name: a valuable piece of information that could be used to compromise her identity on another website.

Public: I think the public figure on Facebook should take some reasonable precautions here to shield any declared relationships from third-parties by isolating any of these options (Relationship Status, Family, and Friends) to a list. Even the public figure on Facebook would want to exercise some caution here. Set each of these to your Circle of Trust.

Guarded: There may be some benefit in declaring relationship statuses for your wife and immediate family, but don't go overboard. Share as little information as possible. Conceal all of this information behind a Circle of Trust setting.

Private: Declare no relationship statuses. There's no functional reason to give this information over to Facebook. If you provide any whatsoever, secure them to Only Me.

Facebook > Timeline > Subscribers (Found Beneath the Cover)

In a recent system update, Facebook has allowed people who're interested in what you have to say to receive your content posted in the public domain without being your friend. This is referred to as a Subscriber. This is an awkward form of relationship that lends some degree of privacy to public figures on Facebook: people can read your public status updates in their news feed and you don't necessarily need to "friend" them. This way we can avoid having zillions of friends even if we're a public figure. Subscribers features are found in a couple of areas on Facebook. On your Facebook Profile, to the left-hand navigation element, there is a Subscribers item. If you click on that item, you'll be brought to a section of your profile depicting people who've expressed an interest in being your friend, but you haven't confirmed them as a friend. Instead, they're subscribed to you. You can then find the Edit Settings in the upper-right hand corner.

Guarded or Private: I'd recommend you turn Subscribers off. You're not a public figure and you've nothing public to say. Also, check the box "Friend Requests" to an on setting. This will only allow friends of your friends to try to "friend" you on Facebook, preventing spam and the chance for unsolicited "friending".

Public: Those who intend to be public figures on Facebook should leave this option on and set Comments and Notifications to Everyone. Why not share your ideas with everyone and allow everyone to comment and forward them inside of their own social networks? When you post content to the general public-at-large, your subscribers will receive this content. If you post something to a list or your friends, they will not receive this content.

Facebook > Timeline > Update Info > Work and Education

Facebook uses information in your Profile to connect you with others. When you indicate your work and education history in Facebook, it gives Facebook an opportunity to connect you with alumni organizations, professional colleagues, past friends, and former teachers and professors who may also be on Facebook.

Private: Providing this information to Facebook makes you more visible and easier to find by others. If your intention is to be a private person on Facebook, you would not want to complete this section of your Profile. Giving Facebook this information makes it easier for the guarded and

public figures on Facebook to network and make connections. It would
make it easier to be found and to find others who're important to you. Still,
there is a significant risk for providing Facebook this information in that – if
it's left in the public domain – anyone can see it. It's kind of like you
decided to print up a zillion copies of your resume and then left stacks of it
at coffee shops, prisons, the mall, a cattle ranch, and a bakery in New Deli.
This is highly sensitive information about you that you've decided to spread
around everywhere. With it, somebody with ill-intent could:

- Attempt to impersonate you on a job or credit application;

- Attempt to acquire your transcripts;

- Attempt to acquire payroll or human resource files about you from
  former employers;

- Learn more about your background as to transgress on others you
  associated with at those institutions;

- Use that information to market specific products and services to
  you.

Guarded: If your intention is to be a guarded person on Facebook, you will
want to limit this information to your Circle of Trust. Only a few trusted folks
should know your entire work and education history. Secure it on your
Profile. Be mindful of the applications that desire access to this information.

Public: Bearing in mind that the public persona on Facebook wants to be
found, you can still work with the system through two tactics: obscurity and
misinformation. Only provide your most recent employer and make that
public, deliberately omitting nearly all of your previous employers. Without

additional information, it'd be difficult to piece together more about you. Further, if you do end up providing a work or academic history, change some of the dates or years you worked or went to school there. Both tactics will help confound the aggressor and secure your presence on Facebook.

Facebook > Timeline > Update Info > Basic Info > Religious and Political Views

In database terminology, a relationship is a connection made between things, or, entities. Those connections can then be used to draw a line between entities, or, entities and things. When Facebook gives its registered users a way to indicate their personal belief systems or philosophy, they're offering a way for people to connect to ideas. It's a software tool used to create relationships between complex ideas and active users.

If we removed the commercialization of Facebook and considered Facebook as simply a tool to build community and to connect with others with like-minded ideas, then Facebook feels palatable. It's connecting us with others who might believe as we do and helps foster stronger friendships. However, for all of the reasons we've discussed, it's difficult to remove the commercial aspect from Facebook, and it's even more difficult to suppress the assumptions third parties could make in accessing this information.

A potential result could be as something as innocuous as a higher frequency for displaying ads for local kosher meats if a Facebook user was to declare themselves of Jewish faith. This would be an outcome Facebook would present as a positive for both the consumer and third-party producer, and Facebook fulfilled its role as a broker within a marketplace of ideas.

Yet it's an entirely different result when that declaration could potentially target that user for potential hate messages; phone or mail harassment from anti-Semitism groups; outright discrimination IRL (In Real Life); cyberbullying; physical violence; and in extreme circumstances - found outright in less democratic societies than the United States – political subjugation. Facebook is a very convenient tool for intolerant political majorities.

Private: If your intention is to be a private persona on Facebook, I see little reason for sharing information about your personal philosophies. Again, it's a way Facebook uses to find you. If you wish not to be found, there's no reason to populate any of this information.

Guarded: What terrifies me most about this setting on Facebook is how it tends towards a naïve worldview, that everyone – everywhere – somehow exists in a vacuum of political persecution; that everyone shares a cultural tradition for sharing the most private and intimate (perhaps spiritual) details of our lives. To me, that reeks of privilege and naivety and inasmuch I feel this is a dangerous setting on Facebook. It presumes we live in a world absent of hate, strong and perhaps violent opinions, cultural biases, or political and ideological aggression. It presumes nobody would think ill of us sharing it, and that they won't use that information in any way against us because people are rational beings. This isn't true. This setting is a badge. And badges got a pretty bad wrap in the second World War, too, for the same reason except this time the badge can be queried immediately by anyone. If you're a guarded personality on Facebook, I'd think twice about providing anything here, and if you do, lock it down to your Circle of Trust.

Public: If you're a public figure on Facebook, use these associations to your advantage by linking to the various interests you're marketing towards. Try to think strategically: what ideas are expressly linked to your brand, your product or services, or even your geographical proximity? Who is your likely demographic? If you're a public figure on Facebook, you want to leverage these relationships to the greatest extent to guarantee the broadest exposure to potential consumers.

Yet sharing your Philosophical leanings as a public figure isn't without risk. Myself, I lean quite left in my politics, and broadcasting that fact on my Facebook Profile might alienate potential clients and dissuade others from working with me. I run the real risk of offending others. It may be more prudent for me to share interests that are specific to my marketing goals on Facebook.

Facebook > Timeline > Likes (Found Beneath the Cover)

Fans are everywhere on Facebook. In fact, Facebook Pages used be called "Fan Pages" because people were "fans" of music artists and celebrities. People like to show their support for their passions on Facebook. Whether or not it's an affinity for the opera, or classical music, the book *Great Expectations*, P. Diddy, or mime, just like under the philosophical relationships you can make with your profile, Facebook wants to present your appreciation for these things like they were badges. Through specifying arts, artists, and venues within this setting, Facebook presumes that you're a fan of these things and wish to connect with others who share similar tastes.

These relationships also have a very useful marketing purpose. If I was using Facebook's advertising platform to market my products and services to you, I could be able to select from a population interested in specific artists or venues who'd likely share an interest in my product. For example, say that I was the producer of a play. I could create a Facebook marketing campaign that targets consumers based on:

- Age

- Gender

- Location (narrowed to my city or 25 miles away from it)

- Income

- Education

- Work History

- Interests (opera, performances, live performances, plays, shows)

The campaign could be generated in minutes and immediately hit thousands of potential consumers. From my perspective (as somebody who wants to sell tickets to my event) this is an awesome capability available only to me on Facebook. A majority of people spend their online time on Facebook and would likely see my ad, too. What a remarkably convenient way to reach-out to a potential patron!

On the other hand, the campaign could be perceived as an intrusion of my privacy. As a patron of the arts, maybe I've already committed my support behind other endeavors and I might feel intruded upon to be approached in this way. Why should Facebook give preference to advertisers and their content based on me being a fan of the arts?

Still, I'm very passionate about one of my favorite bands – the B52's – and I want to know everything about them. I'm a fan! When new content is released from the B52's, I want to know about it, and I'd like it if Facebook facilitated that interaction. Facebook will give preference to content that may be related to my declared interest.

Yet if somebody could generate an advertising campaign knowing that most people who like the B52's also like another artist or cause or product or service, and then they use Facebook to market to me directly, has my interest in the B52's betrayed me? Has my privacy been violated?

Private: Conceivably, the private person on Facebook wouldn't be interested in sharing information with anyone, or in connecting with potential artists or venues. The private person would leave this information blank.

Guarded: Like me, you may have legitimate interests that you want to keep tabs on. You're a fan and you want to keep up with the latest content from your favorite bands and interests. Declaring your affinity for these things may seem like a logical and desirable thing to do in a social space like Facebook. But an ounce of precaution goes a long way. Limit the exposure of your interest to your Circle of Trust, or, only to your friends, and be cautious of applications that wish to access this information.

Public: Opportunity is knocking; can you hear it? Not just to stay in touch with content but to create content and advertising strategies that could be seen by others.

Facebook > Timeline > Update Info > Contact Info

There's a time-honored tradition on the Internet called *scraping*. Programs can be set to read certain kinds of information on websites, capture their text and write them to a file. This process comes in handy if you're interested in email addresses, physical mailing addresses, and telephone numbers – all of which are often freely provided by users on websites, discussion forums, and social networking venues. Scraping is the easiest way to compile an illegal mailing list from information scattered across the web. I say *illegal* because the 2003 Federal Anti-Spam laws prohibit acquiring seed addresses like this, but it's still one of the more effective ways humans on Facebook can commit identity theft. It's as simple as friending, copying, and pasting.

Private: If you're a private person, you likely don't have the desire to share your phone number, email addresses, or mailing address with anyone on Facebook, so don't provide them. Don't enter any of this information. As for your email address used to create your Facebook account, limit displaying that email address to Only Me. In theory, nobody else would need to see it.

Guarded: You may wish to give your Friends access to your email address and mobile numbers, or even your mailing address. Do so by toggling the permissions for each of these items. Provide only the email address you used to create your Facebook account and provide no other. Provide only your authorized mobile number. Obscure your physical address from everyone by limiting it to Only Me.

Public: A little bit of publicity never hurt anybody. Provide as many email addresses as possible to help Facebook match you to friends online! Also, enter your work, home, and mobile numbers that people might have in their address books – this will also help Facebook match you to others. Also enter your mailing address. Make it easy for people to find, contact, and connect with you. If total transparency sounds a bit spooky you can err on the side of caution. If you have skipped ahead and read my COP (Control Online Privacy) suggestions, then you'd know that you could provide an untrusted phone number, an untrusted email address, or, an untrusted mailing address, as a way to protect your real PPI.

Facebook Privacy Settings
Facebook > Privacy Settings > Default Visibility

I believe I've already made it patently clear that when you upload new content to Facebook it's automatically made available to the public. Facebook presumes that nearly everything you post is publically available. That much I'm sure you're aware of. However, in its recent spate of changes, Facebook extended the ability for users to change their default visibility setting away from public and to restrict the visibility of new posts. More specifically, you can customize the privacy setting within Default Visibility to be Public, Friends or Custom, whereas Custom allows you to narrow future updates to a specific List. This setting is global: no matter what device you end up using (your phone, your tablet, or your computer, let's say), your account will post new content in a restricted way to the audience you specify. Further, you can override the default setting when you make a post.

Private: What a boon to the person who wants a private persona on Facebook! Finally, you can set it up so that only your Friends or, say, your Circle of Trust receives your Facebook content. It's an important setting. The private individual would want to change this setting right away to restrict all of their future content to a defined audience.

Although I consider myself a very public person on Facebook, I actually have set my Default Privacy setting to my Circle of Trust. This says that anything that I upload or post to Facebook is private to a select group of people that I know, and if I want to, I can change that setting to include a wider audience at will. I generally believe the presumption of strongest privacy with an option to make content public is the smarter way to go.

Guarded: Maybe you're not crazy about limiting your audience to a List but to your Friends? In this way, the content you upload can be concealed from the general public and available only to Friends. This helps with the future employer problem. The future employer is part of the public and is not a Friend, and they wouldn't have access to see updates and content you upload if you – by default – limited it to your Friends. Still, careful: if this employer suddenly becomes a Friend on Facebook, then they'll have access to your content.

Public: If your intention is to be a public person on Facebook and if you want to be easily found and recognized online, you'd want to leave this setting public. Everything you post is available to everybody else throughout all time.

Facebook > Privacy Settings > How You Connect

How You Connect is broken into five questions:

- *Who can lookup your profile/timeline by name or contact information?* This option controls how active Facebook users can find you on Facebook through lookups and cross-references. Again, this is restricted to an active Facebook user meaning they've got a Facebook account and they're logged-in, using Facebook to find you. Facebook offers only three options for this setting: Everyone, Friends of Friends, or Friends. Unfortunately, you can't restrict this option to a List of your choice. The *Private* person on Facebook would opt for the most restrictive setting (Friends), whereas the *Guarded* person on Facebook would want to limit their ability to be found online. Finally, the *Public* person should have no qualms at all for allowing themselves to be found by Everyone on Facebook.

- *Who can send you Friend requests?* This setting is for anyone who hates being bombarded with Friend Requests from folks you've never heard of. Facebook users can now restrict who can *friend* them to a smaller body of active users. Facebook offers two options for this setting: Everyone or Friends of Friends. The Private person on Facebook would set this to the most restrictive setting (Friends of Friends) which suggests only the people you know and the people they know can *friend* you. The *Guarded* person would probably also want to select the Friends of Friends option if they had already restricted the ability for Everyone to look them up. Otherwise, the *Public* person on Facebook shouldn't have any reason to restrict being found, and would leave this setting as Everyone.

- *Who can send you Facebook messages?* A message in Facebook parlance is a private Facebook email. Messages aren't posted to a user's wall and are only seen by the sender and recipients. Under default conditions, Everyone can send you a Facebook message. You, as a Private person, may not appreciate that, and may wish to restrict this option to a smaller group of active users by setting it to the most restrictive option, *Friends*. Only your Friends can send you direct messages. Guarded persons on Facebook would probably feel comfortable expanding this out to Friends of Friends, while the Public person is available to speak to Everyone in a message. Again, I consider myself a pretty Public person on Facebook but still restrict this option to Friends. Why? Because I don't want any application or unauthorized 3rd party to send me messages in Facebook as spam, or, annoy me with bogus chatter. I feel messages are reserved for people that I know and I'm comfortable with.

- *Who can post on your profile/timeline?* When you or somebody else posts to your wall, if you haven't further restricted Facebook's default behavior (see below, the fifth question) then that post is made available in the newsfeed for all of your friends to see. That could be kind of a problem. It could be a problem because the post could be offensive, it could be spammy, or it could simply be inconvenient or worrisome. Facebook offers two options here: Friends or Only Me. The Private person on Facebook would choose the most restrictive option (Only Me) and prohibit anyone from being able to post to their wall, and this isn't a bad position to take for the Guarded person, either. If you're at all concerned about being embarrassed by content left by others on your profile, then you're likely to set this option to Only Me. If you've a strong constitution, don't mind what people might or might not say to you on your profile, and want to be as social as possible, you'd leave this option available only to your Friends.

- *Who can see posts by others on your profile/timeline?* If you've opted for Only Me on the fourth question, then this option becomes Only Me. That's only fitting: it'd be odd otherwise. However, if you've chosen to allow your Friends to post to your profile/timeline, then you can select who can see that content. Again, the Private person on Facebook has only one option here (Only Me) and it can't be changed – nobody can post to their wall and only they would see the content. Yet the Guarded or Public person on Facebook may have opted to allow Friends to post to their profile which, in turn, demands some restrictions on what's posted here. If you're a Guarded person, I'd actually suggest that your Circle of Trust or Only Me is selected here. This way, you can limit the exposure of something said about you and take it away from the public eye. Finally, if you're a Public person on Facebook and want your profile/timeline to become a sounding board for others, then by all means, leave this option as Public; if you wish to be somewhat cautious, you could at least limit the setting to Friends of Friends.

Facebook > Privacy Settings > How Tags Work

A Facebook Tag is a social bookmark. It points to your Facebook profile/timeline and alerts your Friends of content that's been uploaded that you're tagged in. It's like saying, "Hey look! I'm talking about Russell!" Tags are a way to bring attention to content. If somebody uploads a picture and tags you in that picture, it's a searchable reference that associates that picture to you. Similarly, if you're tagged in a video or in a status update, this content is brought to your attention and to the attention of your Friends who may really want to know, see, or watch such content.
Active Facebook users can tag other profiles manually in Facebook by just typing their name to insert a tag. In some cases, they can reference you directly in a picture. Also, Facebook can perform a form of facial recognition on pictures uploaded by your Friends to automatically tag you in the picture. How convenient! Right. Then again, you may want to control this, and these are the options allowing you to do so.

There are five privacy options related to how Facebook tags you:

- _Timeline/Profile review_. If this setting is flipped on or true, it forces content where you've been tagged in to be reviewed and approved by you before it's added to your timeline/profile. Do note that this setting doesn't prevent tagging from happening; on the contrary, it just allows you to review content that you've been tagged in before it gets incorporated in your timeline/profile. It's a setting to Facebook that you want to review what's said about you before it becomes accessible to your social network.

- _Tag review_. When looking at content and status updates that you've posted, some of your Facebook Friends may wish to tag your content for some other purpose. This setting kind of reminds me of a community scrapbook where everybody standing around some pictures you took and then somebody can point to a picture and say, "Hey, there's Larry!" Everyone's eyes are supposedly drawn to Larry in the photo you took. Maybe you didn't want that; maybe Larry didn't want that; maybe you would feel like the community shouldn't just blurt out who might appear in your scrapbook? That's what this setting allows you to decide. Should your Friends be able to do this or not?

- _Maximum visibility_. If you are tagged in some content uploaded to Facebook, here, Facebook is asking, "What is the maximum reach of content you're tagged in that makes it to your profile/timeline? Who should be able to see that content on your profile?" Example: Circle of Trust. If I said that only my Circle of Trust can see content I'm tagged in, then I'm at least limiting the exposure of potentially embarrassing content to others that I trust. If I left this wide open – Public – then I'd allow anyone who can see my timeline/profile to be able to see that content.

- *Tag suggestions*. When Facebook receives a photo file uploaded by one of your Facebook buddies, it breaks the photo down into a mathematical process. That process looks for faces. Faces have a certain geometry: a symmetry between the eyes, nose, mouth and chin, ears, so they are easily identifiable. And if your face could be broken down into special measurements then those metrics could become a baseline from where new images could be compared. Thus, using facial recognition, Facebook can pick you out in a photograph, or in the least, what Facebook thinks is you, which then Facebook will tag you. Privacy advocates can scream their little hearts out over this one but, really, that's very cool from a social perspective. It automatically identifies folks in your social circle and shares your content. I mean, how cool is that! Yet, maybe you're not into "cool". Maybe you want more control of that process. Maybe you're like me and are more afraid of Facebook committing a "false-positive" tag whereby Facebook tags something that it thinks is me but really isn't. Cool is cool, but do I want Facebook really making assumptions about me? Not really.

- *Tagging through Facebook Places check-ins*. Another interesting feature in Facebook is the ability to tell your social network where you are in the real world. Facebook Places uses the GPS system in your cell phone to report your location through a status update. Interesting information if you think about it. You can let the world know where a great Thai restaurant is and give others a means to meet you there. It's also a way of sharing conveniently through your cell phone. But Places also gives the user the ability to tag Facebook Friends they're with. It's like saying, "Hello World! I'm

here at this Thai restaurant and Mike is with me." Again, cool is
cool, but is this a capability you want to extend to your Friends? Do
you want anyone capable of "checking you in" anywhere in efforts
to let the social network know where you are?

Under each one of these settings we read a bit about our intentions on
Facebook. If your intention is to be a Private person, it's unlikely you'd
want any of these options enabled and you'd might even consider
restricting the Maximum Visibility option to Only Me. That way, you could
entirely control how tags that reference you are displayed on your
timeline/profile.

Meanwhile, if your intention is to be a Guarded person on Facebook, you
might find benefits in tags yet leery of Facebook's Places and facial
recognition features. You may wish to disable those, constraint Maximum
Visibility to your Circle of Trust, and then disable the tag review features.

On the other hand, if you want greater control over the content that can be
tied to your profile, you may want to enable Timeline/Profile Review.
Finally, if your intention is to be as Public a person as possible, then
tagging is a way of life. It allows you to identify others and allows others to
easily identify you. All of these features would be set to the most tolerant
possible.

Facebook > Privacy Settings > Apps Games and Web Sites

Apps You Use. This listing is exactly the same as the applications list we
discussed earlier. If you see an application in this list that you don't
recognize, simply remove it. If you need to, you can always re-authorize it.

How People Bring Your Info Into the Apps They Use. This was one of the more terrifying aspects of Facebook's privacy features. If you select this option, you will see a ginormous list of PPI that can be exposed to Facebook applications used by your Friends, and those applications can access your PPI! Just because your Friend is using it! Imagine for a second that your Friend on Facebook is playing a game and the game looks through your data to see if you'd be a good match to play with them. Yikes! Even worse if the application wasn't necessarily a game but a piece of malware, or, phishing utility. If you're a Private person, you will want to deselect all of these options. If you're a Guarded person and think most of this content is sensitive, deselect all except Website and Current City; this information is fairly public and wouldn't be of much use to anyone. And even if you're a Public person, I would recommend the same. No application used by my friends should have any access to my sensitive PPI, and no application should give third parties access to what I've deemed as confidential.

Instant Personalization. The philosophy behind this setting is referred to in the trade as Single Sign-On (SSO). SSO assumes that you don't want to enter multiple passwords into many websites just to have it recognize you. Instead, what if websites could see a little token from Facebook in the memory of your computer, and that token can be used to authenticate you against Facebook instead of having to re-enter new account information into the website. That's what SSO is all about. You sign-in once to Facebook and Facebook (conveniently again) vouches for your identity to a third party website. Now, your login credential is still stored with Facebook – your actual username and password aren't shared with the third party – so there's no risk of having that information inadvertently lost, exposed, or destroyed. Where there is risk is in the continuity and expiration of that token. If you were to login to Facebook using a computer in a hotel, and then leave without expressly logging-out of Facebook, that token could be used to login as you to other third-party websites. You can see the risk. An unauthorized party could then access other information about you anywhere with only a single credential. SSO increases convenience; it does nothing to increase privacy or security. Private, Guarded, or Public figures on Facebook would do themselves a favor in turning off Instant Personalization.

That said, I'm a Public figure and I have it turned on. Okay, so why? Well, I like having my Facebook account integrated with some of the services that I use online. It makes it easier for me to share information with others, and it simplifies my access of those services. My Facebook picture is shared; I can push content easily to my Friends; I can have the third party website recognize me. So I'm balancing risk versus reward, obviously, and I'm conscious of the risk that I'm taking. My feeling is this: if you're not intending to monitor your Facebook account and its access, and wouldn't know what to look for when it comes to data breaches, then you will want to turn this off.

Public Search. If you enable Public Search, you are allowing Facebook to expose your profile/timeline to search engines. This is the natural, default state of Facebook. If you're a Private or Guarded person, you're likely to deselect this option in favor of constraint. If you're a Public person on Facebook, you're more likely to leave this option selected for you want to have your content indexed and available to search engines. If you're managing an account for a minor child, disabling this option would be a recommended step – conceivably, nothing that a kid has to share with their social network should be searchable content.

Facebook > Privacy Settings > Limit the Audience for Past Posts

Prior to a big security update that Facebook prepared in September 2011, everything you ever posted on Facebook was in the public domain. And presently, if you have never modified this setting before, it is still in the public domain. Ah, clever, no? Facebook gives all of these options to its active users so it can modify the visibility and privacy of future content, but not necessarily tweak the privacy of past content.

Hence we arrive at this feature. This feature allows you to flag all of your previous content to a specific security setting or list. The Public person on Facebook would not be interested in this setting. After all, everything is in the public domain so it can be easily found, exactly as you would want, but if you're a Private or Guarded person on Facebook, you'd want to constrain your past. You'd want to lock it down. That's what this setting allows you to do. You can specify all previous posts and updates get flipped to, say, your Circle of Trust, limiting all of that content's exposure to a specific List. I'd recommend that course of action to any Private or Guarded person on Facebook.

Facebook > Privacy Settings > Blocked People and Apps

The Facebook user interface allows us to block people or applications from interacting with our timeline/profile. Blocking is like a blacklist. We're telling Facebook to not show us their content without "unfriending" them, or, uninstalling the application. We can evaluate and edit that list from this screen.

An example. Farmville. I hate receiving Farmville updates from Friends and I don't have it installed on my profile, but I can still receive status updates from other Friends playing the game. When I block Farmville, I am able to stop receiving updates from it.

Another example. Let's say that I have a friend but I disagree with his politics. I don't wish to "unfriend" him from Facebook – that would just be rude – but I am finding his recent posts obnoxious and tedious. I can block my friend temporarily and then re-enable them later.

If we inadvertently blocked a Friend or an application, we could reinstate their access here. But you can also manage your settings for blocking other Facebook content like events and app invites (where your Friends invite you to play the games they're playing). Enabling any of these features will allow you to create filters for your newsfeed and will diminish the "noise" Facebook generates from others. Ahh, silence.

Facebook also allows you to manage something called a Restricted List. The Restricted List is just a list but it acts as kind of an inverse filter. You can edit this List and add Friends to it, and they would only be able to see content flagged for the public domain. They wouldn't receive anything else. It's a way to keep this party out of the loop without rudely "unfriending" them because users aren't notified when you add them to your Restricted List.

How to Recover from Compromise or Threat

What You Will Learn

- What to do if your account has been hacked on Facebook
- What to do if your friend's account has been hacked on Facebook
- How to delete your Facebook account

What If You've Been Hacked?

Facebook has systems to detect instances of account abuse and they'll shut-down accounts suspected of being compromised. You can read more about this process on Facebook's Account Security Section in the Help Center. If your account is disabled, there's an online process for reclaiming your account, and it can be accessed from here:

http://www.facebook.com/hacked

Following re-activation of your account, you'd want to take an immediate step to change your Facebook password. Use a complex password and then apply some of the privacy and security strategies we've talked about. Thereafter, consider:

1. Don't freak out – there's a recovery process. Follow it.
2. Notify all of your Facebook friends about the situation. Ask for their patience while you sort out the problem with Facebook. Convey that the situation is back under your control.
3. Review the Apps under your Facebook Profile under Facebook's Privacy Settings. Remove any app that isn't essential or that you don't recognize. Remember, apps can be added back later through

re-authorization so it hurts nobody to rip them out and re-authorize them later.

4. Remove the Facebook app from your cell phone and reinstall it, re-authorizing it under your new password.

5. Rotate your password on other critical websites such as financial systems and email systems.

6. Update the security software on your computer and run through a comprehensive scan. Should you work in a professional office space and have a corporate IT function, notify them of the situation and what steps you're taking to correct it.

7. Vigilance. Watch your Facebook, email, and financial accounts for suspicious activity following two weeks of the incident.

What If My Friend Has Been Hacked?

People being people, most will not assume responsibility for their online privacy and security as you have and may not consciously be aware of things should their account be compromised. Unfortunately, their lack of attention to these matters exposes you so there are some steps you can take to help out your buddy and limit your exposure at the same time. Recommendations:

1. Naturally, do not click on anything this friend transmits to you.

2. Remove this friend from your Circle of Trust. That relegates them to a being a public friend with limited access to your PPI.

3. Notify this friend that you suspect their account has been hacked. Forward them a link to Facebook's Account Security Help Center.

4. If this party is a family member or in need of extra assistance, try to help them reclaim their account and rotate their passwords, perhaps walking them through the aforementioned steps.

What if You or Your Friend are Hacked Frequently?

There may come a time where you notice a pattern in account compromises. A friend of yours is constantly having problems managing their account, or, your own account has become the constant target of fraudsters. Take no prisoners here. *Unfriend* your friend until they can get their account under control, and if you're the one whose constantly being victimized, stop the bleeding by killing the patient: delete this Facebook account and start a new one, thereby throwing babies out with bathwaters.

What are Trusted Friends on Facebook?

At the time of this writing, Facebook is attempting to create a new account verification model by recruiting the personal friends of a user to vouch for them. It allows you to designate three to five friends who you trust and who could validate you should your account be compromised. If you've forgotten your password or can't access your email, Facebook will inquire about your legitimacy to these trusted friends who could then pass along an authorization code to you.

Facebook suggests that you can set up trusted friends under **Account > Account Settings > Security** by selecting Trusted Friends. However, at the time of this writing, my own account doesn't have this feature.

It's questionable to me how crowdsourcing account verification in this way will actually make things easier on the common user, but it will make life easier for Facebook who must deal with hundreds of thousands of these cases every day. It shifts verification away from them and onto the backs of your friends which is, well, somewhat cheesy in my opinion. Who wants to be bugged about confirming identity? I believe this feature helps Facebook more than improves the security situation of the consumer.

How to Delete Your Facebook Account

The words "deleting" and "deactivating" are synonymous in this context on Facebook. Deleting an account on Facebook is relatively easy and completely destructive. You can access the Facebook request form online; you can access the deactivation process under **Account Settings > Security**; and more information can be found under Facebook Help. The effect is immediate according to Facebook: all information associated with your profile disappears and your data is permanently removed from their system. There's no recovery option.

If all else fails, deleting a Facebook account and starting over isn't a bad option. Hey, it's just Facebook. Deleting the profile forces Facebook to abandon the special identifiers and keys needed to unlock stuff on Facebook and across the web. Starting fresh may be exactly what's necessary to put yourself in a stronger security position. Use it with care though. Permanent is permanent, and even though you may have downloaded your profile data for safekeeping, there's no mechanism to upload your profile and regenerate it. You'll be starting from scratch.

How to Protect Your PPI Online

What You Will Learn

- Basic Steps to Protect Your Personal Private Information (PPI)
- Conclusion
- Online Resources and Tools

Basic Ways to Protect Your Personal Private Information (PPI)

After reading this book, you've now taken some reasonable precautions to protect your personal private information on Facebook, yet you may still be interested in doing a few more rational things to reduce your exposure online. A while ago, I created a template for discussing security and privacy for my undergraduate classes on Internet Security, and I called these my COP (Control Online Privacy) Methods: simple ways to reduce your risk online. Here are my suggestions:

- Setup at least two email addresses – one that is trusted and the other untrusted; never give out your trusted email address to anyone but friends and family. Protect the trusted email account! Only give it to people you know and trust.

- Setup at least two phone numbers – one that is trusted and the other untrusted; never give out your trusted phone number to anyone but friends and family. Google Voice can be used to obtain a free telephone number. Protect the trusted phone number! Only give it to people you know and trust.

- Do not voluntarily reveal Personal Private Information (PPI) anywhere, to anyone. If you must, use fake information like your untrusted email addresses and phone numbers.

- Setup a special credit card for online purchases and travel. Monitor it and set up the maximum level of alerts on its use through your bank. Get the maximum fraud prevention on it. This card will be your proverbial canary for identity theft.

- Limit online shopping and use of online services to big reputable firms.

- Send all of your mail to a PO Box or a UPS Store. Physical unlocked mailboxes are simply unsecure. Go paperless on all critical accounts and relationships. Avoid sending anything meaningful in terms of PPI in physical mail.

- Shred all documents that contain PPI. Fireproof safes and setup off-site storage for critical documents like insurance policies, licenses, and certificates.

- Never leave your wallet, your purse, or your cell phone anywhere or with anyone. Even the people you'd regularly trust. Be paranoid. Keep them with you at all times.

- Don't sign your credit cards. Force merchants to verify your signature against your driver's license or another piece of ID you carry.

- Use critical thought: think carefully about how you respond to text messages, email, or Facebook posts that incite emotion. People who want to hack you desire to play off of your emotions and skirt your rational response to problems. Beware.

- There is no guarantee of privacy whatsoever at your workplace so don't assume as such. Check your use of email and phone conversations.

- Never reply to spammers. Do not voluntarily put yourself on do-not-call lists. Do not ask to be removed from such lists. These actions only get you placed on more lists.

- Always use encryption.

- Avoid using thumb drives. Use cloud services like Dropbox instead.

- Lock your mobile devices. Lock-down, restrict, or disable geo-location services.

- Do not download files or programs of any kind unless you know where they came from, and, you understand their purpose. Period. If you don't, seek the advice of a professional.

- Turn off instant messaging. If you must use it, use IM with only a select group of people you know and trust. IM offers a direct way to attack your computer, bypassing many controls that systems professionals use to safeguard it from viruses and malware.

- Use complex passwords. Use different passwords everywhere. Rotate your passwords maybe twice a year. Remember that hackers are counting on you to be lazy and lean towards predictability and convenience. Be inconvenienced.

- Limit your "attack profile": close all non-essential social networking accounts. Use filters and lists to control your content.

- Hide your birthday on Facebook. Limit it only to your Circle of Trust, and plug in a birthday different from your actual birthday.

- Obscure your PPI to avoid having your information harvested. Conceal your phone number and address by exposing them only to your Circle of Trust.

- Don't use your full name on any social networking site.

- Use Pages to channel conversations and relationships to a non-personal audience, and use your Facebook Profile to channel conversations and relationships personally to you.

- Do not complete the information in your Facebook Profile related to Education and Work, or, significantly restrict access to it. It could be used to construct a resume or research your past.

- Target all content to specific audiences and avoid public posting on Facebook.

- Flirting romantically with strangers on any social networking site is simply dangerous. Social networking sites of all stripes are hunting grounds for predatory aggressors, including Facebook. Should you wish to meet people you've met on social networks IRL (In Real Life), choose a daylight hour; choose a public place; tell others

where you're going and when you expect to be back; tell others
who you're meeting.

- Teach your kids about privacy and security ... then isolate them to
  their own computers and devices; get them their own accounts.
  And if they can't have an account on their own? Tough.

- Report all suspicious behavior.

Conclusion

The US Forest Service has a mascot named Smokey the Bear who is very
fond of suggesting that only you can prevent forest fires. You're probably
familiar with Smokey and his message. Smokey is an advocate for
personal responsibility and reminds us all of the dire consequences should
we fail in taking reasonable precautions to stay safe.

When it comes to securing your digital life, the same is true. Only you can
secure your PPI. Nobody else is going to do it for you and the systems and
social networks that we use are designed to exploit your PPI as a product.
Consumers are eight times more likely to become the victim of identity theft
following a data breach, and social networks like Facebook exist primarily
to share your PPI with other organizations. Data breaches are likely to rise
and not fall, and given the absence of a strong federal mandate, more data
breaches will go ignored, under-reported, and under-investigated.

Hackers today are driven by greed more so than by vanity or a desire to
permanently destroy your computer system. Instead, they use their
understanding of computer systems to profit from the naivety of end-users
and exploit social networks that encourage everyone to share everything
and to play nice. They don't wish to break your computer. They're more

interested in capturing and reselling information about you. They are wolves overlooking a vast valley of lambs. The predator will continue to attack the prey because the opportunities are bountiful, and because there are limited countermeasures that expose them to risk of being caught or prosecuted. They will always seek out the companies and individuals who're complacent and foolish who fail to take reasonable precautions to protect themselves.

No software will ever save you. No setting from Facebook – aside from deleting your account – will ever completely reduce your risk. There's no overnight solution that can be offered by consultants or security professionals to companies to maintain system confidentiality. There's no magic pill that you can take to be able to make you more secure. It is only by modifying your behaviors, adjusting your expectations, designing inconvenience, and setting appropriate safeguards, will save yourself from fraud and identity theft.

Online Resources and Organizations

- Federal Trade Commission — www.OnGuardOnline.gov - 1-877-FTC-HELP (1-877-382-4357)
- GetNetWise — www.getnetwise.org
- Internet Keep Safe Coalition — www.iKeepSafe.org
- i-SAFE — www.i-safe.org
- National Crime Prevention Council — www.ncpc.org
- National Cyber Security Alliance — www.staysafeonline.org
- Wired Safety — www.wiredsafety.org
- Staysafe — www.staysafe.org

References

1. Meyers, Steve. (September 14, 2011). "Americans Spend Just a Fraction of Online Time With News as Compared to Social Media." Retrieved From URL: http://www.poynter.org/latest-news/romenesko/145736/americans-spend-just-a-fraction-of-online-time-with-news-compared-to-social-media/

2. No author. (2012). Facebook Newsroom. Retrieved From URL: https://www.facebook.com/press/info.php?statistics

3. Qualman, Erik. (September 16, 2011). "Social Networks User Statistics." Retrieved From URL: http://www.socialnomics.net/2011/08/16/social-network-users-statistics/

4. No author. (2012). Facebook Newsroom. Retrieved From URL: www.facebook.com/press/info.php?statistics

5. No author. (May 11, 2010). "The Hidden Dangers of Facebook." Retrieved From URL: http://www.cbsnews.com/stories/2010/05/08/earlyshow/saturday/main6469373.shtml

6. Watters, Audry. (May 20, 2011). "Mark Zuckerberg Wants Kids Under 13 to Join Facebook, Uses Bogus COPPA Excuse to Justify Why They Can't." Retrieved From URL: http://www.hackeducation.com/2011/05/20/mark-zuckerberg-wants-kids-under-13-to-join-facebook-uses-bogus-coppa-excuse-to-justify-why-they-cant/

7. No author. (2011). "Understanding Federal and State Privacy Laws." Retrieved From URL: http://www.bbbonline.org/understandingprivacy/library/fed_stateprivlaws.pdf

8. ibid.

9. Jones, Soltren. (December 14, 2005). "Facebook: Threats to Privacy." Retrieved From URL:

http://groups.csail.mit.edu/mac/classes/6.805/student-papers/fall05-papers/facebook.pdf

10. Wasserman, Todd. (October 21, 2011). "Facebook Says 600,000 Accounts Compromised Per Day." Retrieved From URL:

http://mashable.com/2011/10/28/facebook-600000-accounts-compromised/

11. *ibid.*

12. Arrington, Michael. (July 5, 2010). "Employees Challenged to Crack Facebook Security, Succeeded." Retrieved From URL:

http://techcrunch.com/2010/07/05/employees-challenged-to-crack-facebook-security-succeed/

13. No author. (May 11, 2010). "Five Hidden Dangers of Facebook." Retrieved From URL:

http://www.cbsnews.com/stories/2010/05/08/earlyshow/saturday/main6469373.shtml

14. No Author. (2011). "Six Facebook Privacy Blunders." Retrieved From URL:

http://www.itbusinessedge.com/slideshows/show.aspx?c=91471&slide=2

15. *ibid.*

16. No author. (May 11, 2010). "Five Hidden Dangers of Facebook." Retrieved From URL:

http://www.cbsnews.com/stories/2010/05/08/earlyshow/saturday/main6469373.shtml

17. Holtz, Alexander. (August 25, 2010). "Facebook Privacy: Six Years of Controversy." Retrieved From URL:

http://mashable.com/2010/08/25/facebook-privacy-infographic/

18. *ibid.*

19. *ibid.*

20. Warren, Christina. (April 18, 2011). "Security Firm: Facebook Should Better Protect Its Users." Retrieved From URL: http://mashable.com/2011/04/18/sophos-facebook-open-letter/

21. No author. (2012). No Title. Retrieved From URL: https://www.facebook.com/about/timeline

22. No author. (2012). The Information Technology & Innovation Foundation. "Innovation Fact of the Week." Retrieved From URL: http://www.itif.org/content/2010-81-million-americans-were-victims-identity-theft-losses-totaling-37-billion

23. *ibid.*

24. *ibid.*

25. *ibid.*

26. No author. (September 22, 2011). "BBB Advice on College Student Security." Retrieved From URL: http://easternnc.bbb.org/article/bbb-advice-on-college-student-security-29638

27. No Author. (March 10, 2011). "Risk of Identity Theft Higher for Social Network Users." Retrieved From URL: http://www.myid.com/blog/risk-for-identity-theft-high-for-social-network-users/

28. Chairman Bill Thomas. (July 7, 2004). Committee on Ways and Means. "Facts and Figures: Identity Theft." Retrieved From URL: http://waysandmeans.house.gov/media/pdf/ss/factsfigures.pdf

29. Siciliano, Robert. (July 23, 2009). "Identity Theft Committed Using Social Networks." Retrieved From URL:

http://www.huffingtonpost.com/robert-siciliano/identity-theft-commited-u_b_243305.html

30. *ibid.*

31. *ibid.*

32. No Author. (March 10, 2011). "Risk of Identity Theft Higher for Social Network Users." Retrieved From URL: http://www.myid.com/blog/risk-for-identity-theft-high-for-social-network-users/

33. *ibid.*

34. No author. (May 11, 2010). "Five Hidden Dangers of Facebook." Retrieved From URL: http://www.cbsnews.com/stories/2010/05/08/earlyshow/saturday/main6469373.shtml

www.ingramcontent.com/pod-product-compliance
Lightning Source LLC
Chambersburg PA
CBHW052147070326
40689CB00050B/2414

Facebook is one of the most popular destinations on the Internet: Americans spend nearly a quarter of their online time there. And while using Facebook, volumes of their personal private information is voluntarily exposed to marketers, fraudsters, and hackers. Regrettably, very few understand the risks and even fewer users know what settings to flip to make their profile more secure on Facebook.

This book is for the enlightened business owner, engaged parent, inquisitive teen, or concerned consumer who're looking to understand their risks in using Facebook, and, what buttons to flip to better lock-down their profile. This book offers a 30,000-foot perspective on the risks facing every Facebook user yet zooms-in on specific actions, settings, and configurations to make Facebook's privacy settings work for you.

Russell Mickler, Principal Consultant of Mickler & Associates, Inc., has over 17 years of professional experience leading and managing IT organizations. As a technology consultant, Mickler assists small to mid-range businesses with crafting and executing technology strategy. In addition to earning his Master's Degree in technology from the University of Oregon, Mickler is a Computer Information Systems Security Professional (CISSP) and a Microsoft Certified Systems Engineer (MCSE). Mickler teaches graduate and undergraduate technology courses for many universities across the country. Mickler is the co-author of several books concerning Information Technology and Information Security. Mickler is also a public speaker on matters concerning social media and technology, and creates all types of media at micklerandassociates.com and his blog reinventwork.com. Russell Mickler and Mickler & Associates, Inc. can be found on Facebook, on Twitter at @micklerr, and emailed directly at russell@simple-books.net.

ISBN 9780983524113

90000 >

9 780983 524113